*Greek
Philosophers
of the
Hellenistic
Age*

PAUL OSKAR KRISTELLER

Authorized English Translation by Gregory Woods

Greek
Philosophers
of the
Hellenistic
Age

New York : Columbia University Press

Columbia University Press

New York   Oxford

Filosofi greci dell'età ellenistica: copyright © 1991

Scuola Normale Superiore, Pisa

English translation copyright © 1993 Paul Oskar Kristeller

Library of Congress Cataloging-in-Publication Data

Kristeller, Paul Oskar, 1905–
[Filosofi greci dell'età ellenistica.   English]
Greek philosophers of the Hellenistic age / Paul Oskar
Kristeller : authorized English translation by Gregory Woods.
p.   cm.
Translation of: Filosofi greci dell'età ellenistica.
Includes bibliographical references.
ISBN 0–231–07952–4
1. Philosophy, Ancient.   I. Title.
B505.K7513   1993
182—dc20   92–32482
CIP

Printed in the United States of America

c 10 9 8 7 6 5 4 3 2 1

To the memory of Enrico De Negri

CONTENTS

Preface to the
American Edition

When I wrote my lectures on Hellenistic Philosophy and delivered them in 1989 at the Scuola Normale Superiore in Pisa
under the auspices of the Accademia Nazionale dei Lincei, it
was understood that they would be published in Italian by the
Scuola itself. I welcomed the opportunity to treat in these
lectures a subject on which I had lectured many times at
Columbia University, but published very little. Since there are
few studies in English that deal with the subject in the same
way, as to context, emphasis, and interpretation, many of my
American friends and former students insisted that the Italian

edition should be followed, as soon as possible, by an English version that would find in this country and elsewhere, among scholars as well as students, a larger audience than might be expected of the Italian edition. The Columbia University Press agreed to publish the English version, and the translation was entrusted to Dr. Gregory Woods, a former student of mine. I examined his translation rather carefully, and am glad to approve it as the authorized translation of my little volume.

I wish to thank Dr. Woods for his careful and painstaking work, and the Columbia University Press, especially Mr. John Moore and Ms. Ann Miller, for their willingness to publish this book in its present form.

The English typescript, submitted to the press on a disk by Dr. Woods, has been copyedited rather carefully by Ms. Joan McQuary, Ms. Anne McCoy, and Mr. Roy Thomas. I have gone over their suggestions in great detail and am glad to state that we have accepted many of them or have revised and clarified many previous passages that may give rise to misunderstandings.

The passages of the ancient authors, as they are cited in our text, with the exception of Cicero's *Orator* and a few other authors available in the Loeb Library or a few other standard translations, are given in our own translation—that is, in Dr. Woods' translation, revised by me and derived from the Italian translation made by me for the Pisa edition. This English translation, as well as my connecting text, will make this volume, to be sure, accessible and useful for college seniors and graduate students. Yet the notes in which we cite, or refer to, the standard editions of the original Greek (or Latin) texts, along with our translation and with the bibliography, should also be useful and interesting for the scholarly specialist who may, if he wishes, compare our translation and interpretation with the sources on which it is based, and thus judge the accuracy and validity of our work by the only criterion I accept in the study of the history of philosophy—namely, its agreement with the original texts of the fragments and testimonies that are at our disposal. The editions of the fragments and testimonies usually contain no translations, and when they do contain translations or even English translations (as may happen in a few instances), I never base my interpretation on these translations, but only on the original texts as printed.

The bibliography contains only titles dealing with Hellenistic philosophy, including some that are not cited in the notes. Vice versa, some titles cited in the notes are not repeated in the bibliography because they do not concern Hellenistic philosophy but only its earlier sources or later influences.

I am indebted for their competent help to Mr. Andrew Gregory, and to the Reference Department of Columbia's Butler Library, who verified for me most of the publishers of the books, originally cited by me only by place and date.

New York, Columbia University
September 1992

Preface to the
Italian Edition

The eight Comparetti Lectures brought together in this small
book were delivered at the Scuola Normale Superiore in Pisa
under the auspices of the Accademia Nazionale dei Lincei in
April and May of 1989. I should like to thank these two illustrious institutions for their invitation. In part my presentation
is based on a course on Greek philosophy after Aristotle given
at Columbia University a number of times, as well as in Pisa on
one occasion. For certain parts of the final lectures I made use
of a small thesis that I wrote in Berlin in 1929, which I have
since reworked as an essay published in Heidelberg in 1989.

I also want to thank Professor Giuseppe Nenci and Professor Emilio Peruzzi for their help in the editing of these lectures.

To some degree I have followed the method of presentation in eight lectures that I adopted at Stanford University in 1961. These lectures were published in 1964 under the title *Eight Philosophers of the Italian Renaissance.* I realize that specialists on this subject may not agree with everything I have to say, and in particular, my polemical remarks will not please everyone. If there are some repetitions, especially in my presentations on Zeno and Chrysippus, I apologize for them as unavoidable for the sake of coherence, since each lecture was meant to be an independent unit. I hope that readers will not mind these repetitions or at least that they will excuse them. The notes refer principally to the primary sources I have used. The bibliography is indispensable for those who wish to study the subject in greater depth, but it has not been my intention to quote secondary works in the notes or to discuss in the text all particular questions that have been topics of learned controversy. I admit that I may have neglected to deal with some important problems, but there are good reasons for my choice of the interpretations that I present.

New York, December 31, 1990

Greek
Philosophers
of the
Hellenistic
Age

CHAPTER ONE

Epicurus

Mr. Director, Colleagues and Friends, Students and Guests,

First of all, I wish to thank the authorities of the Scuola Normale Superiore, an institution with which I have been closely associated for many years, as well as the authorities of the Accademia Nazionale dei Lincei, of which I am a corresponding member, for the great honor of inviting me to deliver the Comparetti Lectures this year and so to inaugurate a series of lectures that other scholars will carry on for many years to come. For me the invitation is the source of special satisfaction, as it gives me the opportunity to finish my teaching career here in the very same Pisa where it had its beginnings more than half a century ago. I am pleased as well to see that also in Italy you have taken up this kind of series of regular public lectures, which has been customary in England and America for some time. These are well suited to a concise and summary, yet comprehensible, presentation of a complex topic, leaving aside minor issues and controversies. I shall try to use this method to advantage, basing these lectures on primary sources rather than on recent critical literature (which I do not claim to know completely anyway), and in part using a course that I gave several times at Columbia University and once, in 1952, at the Scuola Normale, but never published.

Ancient philosophy from Thales, Plato, and Aristotle to Plotinus, Proclus, Simplicius, and St. Augustine has been, and continues to be, a primary subject for all who study philosophy and the history of philosophy—indeed, for all those interested in the thought and culture of the West of which it is a central and enduring part. From this ancient philosophical tradition most of the works of Aristotle—and all those of Plato and Plotinus—have been completely preserved, along with many works by other philosophers or popular writers, Roman, Jewish, Christian, and Neo-Platonic. In these works are preserved the fragments of and references to other authors whose writings are either entirely or substantially lost. The Hellenistic authors we are to deal with do not survive. Their thought, like that of the Pre-Socratics, must be reconstructed from the fragments and summaries preserved by later authors. They were carefully assembled by modern scholars whose work is like that of the archaeologists who reconstruct the cities and monuments of Antiquity out of ruins either preserved or unearthed. Since the time allotted to us is brief in relation to our subject, we have to limit ourselves to the period that goes from the death of Aristotle to the middle of the first century before Christ, leaving out the Pre-Socratics, Socrates, Plato, and Aristotle on the one side and the Platonic, Aristotelian, Stoic, and Skeptic authors of the first two centuries of our era on the other. I have also left out all Roman, Jewish, and Christian authors along with all the neo-Platonic thinkers. Even within the limited time period we are treating, we must leave aside many important thinkers like those of the Socratic schools, the first successors of Plato, and the whole Aristotelian tradition. We shall focus only on Epicurus, on Early and Middle Stoicism, and on the later Academy of the Skeptics and the eclectic thinkers.

Even regarding the thinkers of whom we speak we must confine ourselves to a few doctrines that are characteristic of their thinking, or are significant philosophically or historically, or that have simply aroused my curiosity. I must also excuse myself if I talk on subjects that many scholars, perhaps even some here in this hall, know better than I. However, I do not subscribe to the now widely held opinion that the thought of the past has no importance for today's world and is no more than the by-product of psychological, political, economic, and social factors that are neither defined nor documented—whereas the alleged irresistible force of these ideas is never applied to the type of thinking that passes as fashionable today. I consider the philosophical thought from Thales to Hegel and beyond rather as a rich treasury of interesting and partly valid ideas which merit interpretation and rethinking and have left their traces in the philosophical and ordinary everyday vocabulary that we use today and whose origins deserve to be explored. Moreover, I like to examine the neglected periods of our philosophical tradition whose importance and influence have been undervalued, denied, or even forgotten in the wake both of a widespread dogmatism now rampant in philosophy, theology, and ideology and of the profound ignorance that is its cause and effect.

In order to understand Hellenistic thought, one must be

mindful of the place that philosophy and the teaching of it held in the culture of the period. The four schools founded in Athens by Plato, Aristotle, Zeno, and Epicurus were organized and lasting institutions, with buildings, with elected heads or scholarchs, with an established program, and with a more or less fixed doctrine. Athens became a university city, drawing students from the entire ancient world, and served as a model for other younger and less permanent centers, like Alexandria and Rome. The coexistence of rival schools favored a teaching method we might call scholastic, and this led each school to defend its position with new arguments and to refute the arguments of the other schools, to maintain its orthodox tradition, but also to absorb, in a more or less eclectic fashion, some of the teachings or arguments of the rival schools. Another characteristic development separated the teaching of philosophy into three parts—logic, physics, and ethics (a division apparently introduced by Xenocrates)—with the result that, at least in the schools of the Stoics and the Epicureans, ethics became the end and the center of all philosophical teaching. Philosophy itself was conceived of not only as universal knowledge but also as the art of living. Following the example of Aristotle, the philosophical schools often included rhetoric in their program, and hence were in competition with the numerous and widespread schools of rhetoric. The schools of philosophy drew great numbers of students from all parts of the Hellenistic and Roman world, and generally these students were not philosophers by profession, but rather cultured persons who gained distinction in the political or professional arena and spread the ideas of their teachers in their own writings and activities. As a result, philosophy and the teaching of philosophy had a greater public and a deeper influence on general culture during the Hellenistic period than at almost any other time in the history of the Western world.

Epicurus, to whom we dedicate this first lecture, was born in 342 B.C., founded his school (which assembled in the garden of his residence in Athens) about 306, and died in 270. This school lasted for many centuries down to the end of classical Antiquity, and its teachings in this long period underwent fewer changes than was the case in the other philosophical schools. The school of Epicurus has many aspects of a religious community. Its doctrine was itself understood as a road toward individual happiness, and teacher and disciples were bound to each other by a special bond of friendship. Epicurus addressed many doctrinal and personal letters (some of which are preserved) to his disciples and friends, thus inaugurating the philosophical epistle as a literary genre. In these letters, and in the collections of his principal sayings, we can appreciate the originality and personality of his style.[1] His successors, including Lucretius and Philodemus, remained substantially faithful to the teaching of the master, and Epicureanism preserved a uniform and orthodox tradition for many centuries. On the other hand, Epicureanism was bitterly attacked and criticized by the other schools—especially by the Stoics, by Cicero, and by many Christian authors—and in the course of these polemics Epicurus' teaching was itself often misrepresented. His adversaries attributed to Epicurus a vulgar hedonism far removed from his authentic doctrine, and this misconception has continued in the popular image of Epicurus until today. Curiously, the vulgar and misconstrued Epicureanism found in Cicero was defended and praised by

---

1. The principal source on Epicurus is Diogenes Laertius, *Vitae et Placita philosophorum*, book 10. For the texts and fragments, see *Epicurea*, ed. H. Usener; *Epicuro: Opere*, ed. G. Arrighetti; *Epicurus: Epistulae tres et Ratae Sententiae*, ed. P. von der Muehll; and *Epikur: Brief an Pythokles*, ed. E. Boer.

Lorenzo Valla in his *De vero bono*, with Valla actually coming out in favor of the very caricature of Epicureanism attacked by the Stoics and the Church Fathers. In fact, Epicurus had little influence on neo-Platonic, patristic, and medieval philosophy. Starting with the Quattrocento, the epistemological, physical, and moral ideas of Epicurus and Lucretius were taken up and adopted by many philosophers and scientists like Ficino and Bruno, Galileo and Gassendi. In modern times his empiricism, materialism, and hedonism have often been more admired than understood, while the scholarly bibliography on Epicurus and his school has been rich and includes the literature on the Philodemus papyri from Herculaneum. These papyri have added since the Quattrocento many new fragments to those previously well known from Diogenes Laertius and other ancient authors.

The doctrine of Epicurus, like that of the Stoics, is divided into three parts: logic, physics, and ethics. The logic that Epicurus calls canonic and reduces to a purely introductory function deals mostly with the criterion of truth.[2] Epicurus holds that the only foundation for knowledge is phantasy or perception (*phantasia*) and that every phantasy is based directly on an object (*phantaston*) which exists in reality (*huparkhei*). Phantasy, therefore, is always true, and if differing perceptions of the same object seem to be contrary to one another, it simply means that every phantasy is a different aspect of the same complex object, or that the difference comes not from the perceptions themselves but from the opinions based on them. General concepts that do not correspond to a direct perception are explained through the memory of repeated particular perceptions, and this memory leads to the anticipation of an

2. Usener, fr. 29 and 242; and Arrighetti, p. 171.

evident concept (*prolepsis,* a term coined by Epicurus precisely for this purpose). The general concept thus is not based directly on the perception of a real object, but results from repeated particular perceptions, and it becomes valid because each person arrives from the same repeated perceptions to the formation of the same general concepts. From phantasy or perception (*phantasia*) we must distinguish opinion (*doxa*), that is, every theoretical affirmation on any object. According to Epicurus, the truth and validity of an opinion is never intrinsic but is based entirely on perceptions and their objects. An opinion is true when it is confirmed and not refuted by perception, and is false when it is refuted or not confirmed by perception.[3] What we have here is a simple and convincing theory of empirical knowledge. (It is definitely not adequate for a priori knowledge.) But Epicurus' theory is sufficient for empirical and, especially, for historical knowledge. As historians and philologists, we must base ourselves on texts and documents, and our opinions are valid inasmuch as they correspond to the evidence; if they do not correspond, they are invalid. In the methodology of the historical and philological sciences, I gladly follow a transformed version of the epistemology of Epicurus. And I heartily recommend it to those colleagues who are in sympathy with the empiricism and materialism of Epicurus, but who do not feel they need to base themselves on the evidence of known facts and of authenticated texts and documents.

Still more important and of more enduring influence is the physics of Epicurus, which is based mainly, though not en-

3. Usener, fr. 247 (Sextus Empiricus, *Adversus mathematicos* 7.203–16); and Arrighetti, fr. 151. See also Usener, fr. 250 (Plutarch, *Adversus Colotem,* 4–5); Arrighetti, fr. 152; and *Epist.* 1.51.

tirely, on the doctrine of Democritus. Also for Epicurus nature consists only of bodies (*somata*) and of the void (*kenon*).[4] The existence of bodies is attested to by sensation, and the existence of the void is necessary for the explanation of motion. Outside of the void and of bodies nothing exists but their accidents.[5] This position is also based on some universal axioms (e.g., nothing can be generated from nothing, and no being can be completely destroyed or reduced to nothing). The universe has always been the same as it is now and will always be the same, since there is nothing outside of it.[6] Bodies consist of atoms and their combinations, and the universe is infinite with respect both to the multitude of atoms and to the extent of the void.[7] Atoms have different shapes, and the number of those with the same shape is infinite, while the number of different shapes is not infinite but simply undefinable.[8] Atoms are in constant motion and, being solid, they constantly collide with one another.[9] There are infinite worlds, some of them similar to ours and some dissimilar.[10] Solid bodies produce in the air images (*eidola*) or emanations (*aporroiai*),[11] and these images encounter our organs and produce our perceptions and phantasies.[12] Atoms are not infinitely divisible since they have a limited size.[13] Atoms have

4. Usener, fr. 74 and 75; and Arrighetti, fr. 23.
5. *Epist.* 1.39–40.
6. *Epist.* 1.38–39.
7. *Epist.* 1.40–41.
8. *Epist.* 1.42.
9. *Epist.* 1.43–44.
10. *Epist.* 1.45.
11. *Epist.* 1.46.
12. *Epist.* 1.49–50.
13. *Epist.* 1.56, 59.

none of the qualities perceived by us, but only shape, size, and gravity.[14]

In this final formula we note an important point where the physics of Epicurus differs from that of Democritus and corrects it. Democritus attributes to the atom as fundamental qualities only size and shape. Thus he conceives of the physical body only as a mathematical being. Epicurus, instead, adds a third attribute to the physical body which corresponds to its physical (and not merely mathematical) properties and he calls this third attribute gravity (*baros*) or resistance (*antitupia*). Our sources (Sextus Empiricus and the doxographers) clearly attest to this doctrine, and one of them states explicitly that it represents an addition to Democritus by Epicurus.[15] In the conven-

---

14. *Skhematos kai barous kai megethous.*

15. Usener, fr. 275 (Plutarch, *De placitis philosophorum* 1.3, 18; Diels, *Doxographi graeci*, pp. 285–86; Sextus Empiricus, *Adv. math.* 10.240, 257). See also Arrighetti, fr. 162. Plutarch states explicitly that Democritus only knew two attributes of the atom—size and shape—and that Epicurus added gravity (*baros*) and resistance (*antitupia*).

For the use of the term *antitupia* in Epicurus, see H. Usener, *Glossarium Epicureum*, ed. M. Gigante and W. Schmid, p. 76. The term is documented in Democritus only once and in an unclear way (*Die Fragmente der Vorsokratiker*, ed. and trans. H. Diels and W. Kranz, 11th ed. [Zurich and Berlin: Weidmann, 1964], vol. 2, p. 101, no. 68, Democritus A 66, from Aetius 1:26, 2: Doxographi Graeci, p. 321). For the meaning of *antitupia* as "resistance," *A Greek-English Lexicon*, ed. Liddell, Scott, Jones (Oxford: Oxford University Press, 1966), p. 165, cites Philodemus, Sextus, Epicurus, Plutarch, and still later authors. The *Thesaurus Linguae Graecae* (computerized printout), ed. Theodore F. Brunner et al., adds Chrysippus, Galen, and many other authors, but no one prior to Epicurus. Hence, it is probable that Epicurus coined this term to express one of his original concepts.

tional descriptions of the Epicurean system, either this point is not underscored or it is not mentioned. But it had a great intrinsic importance and was taken up by the philosophers and scientists of the sixteenth and seventeenth centuries. The theory of resistance was adopted by Francesco Patrizi to distinguish a physical body from a mathematical one, and the Cartesian theory that identifies the body with extension was criticized precisely on this point by Leibniz and Newton and modified and corrected by the addition of a different factor, namely force or gravity.

In the world which is all material, even the soul is but a subtle body that is diffused within the heavier body and is capable of perception.[16] Those who say that the soul is incorporeal are mistaken, since the only thing in the world that is without body is the void, which can neither act nor suffer.[17] Among the accidents of the body some are permanent and others are simply temporary.[18] Time itself is only a temporary quality of motion.[19]

All the particular beings and worlds had a beginning and will come to an end,[20] and only the infinite universe of which they are a part is eternal. All natural phenomena, heavenly or earthly, are explained by natural causes, but in many cases it is necessary and permissible to propose several alternative explanations.[21] Disagreeing with Democritus, Epicurus admits

16. Usener, fr. 310–315, 336–341 (unless otherwise noted, all future Usener references are to *Epicurea*). See also Arrighetti, fr. 158–160; and *Epist.* 1.63.

17. *Epist.* 1.67.

18. *Epist.* 1.68–70.

19. *Epist.* 1.72–73; Usener, fr. 79 and 294; and Arrighetti, fr. 164.

20. *Epist.* 1.73.

21. *Epist.* 2.97.

that atoms are not determined by fixed causes but are subject to chance, and that they can deviate or swerve from their direct movement.[22] Epicurus can explain in this way both free will and the origin of the finite worlds. On this point contemporary physics has abandoned its classical determinism and moved closer to Epicurus' position.

The soul is mortal and is born and dies with the body,[23] and stories about future life are nothing but myths.[24] The same goes for the popular gods and the tales told about them. Nevertheless, there are gods who really do exist and whose existence is confirmed by our valid anticipation (*prolepsis*).[25] They are blessed and eternal, have human shape, live in the intervening spaces between the heavenly spheres, and care nothing about earthly events or human affairs.[26] Therefore, the world is not governed by providence or by fate, but by chance (*automatismos*), and there are no final causes.[27] The philosopher should follow the religious practices of his country, but is undisturbed by popular opinions in his more serious convictions.[28] We learn from Lucretius that Epicurus developed a very pragmatic doctrine of natural and human history in which man progresses step by step from a primitive condition to the life of civilization and culture whose characteristics are family, language and the arts, society, and the state.[29]

The epistemology and logic and the physics of Epicurus,

22. Usener, fr. 281; also, cf. fr. 379.
23. Usener, fr. 336.
24. Usener, fr. 341.
25. Usener, fr. 352.
26. *Epist.* 3.123–24; Usener, fr. 352, 356, 359; Arrighetti, fr. 176.
27. Usener, fr. 359, 368, 370, 383.
28. Usener, fr. 387; Arrighetti, fr. 114.
29. Lucretius, 5.925–1457.

despite their intrinsic and historical importance, serve in his system only as the prologue and foundation for his ethics, which is the central part of his philosophy. For Epicurus, as for all the Greek philosophers, the end of life consists in happiness (*eudaimonia*), but for him and his school the essential element of happiness is pleasure (*hedone*), and the ethical position of the Epicureans is rightly characterized as hedonism. Ethical hedonism has had many followers from antiquity to today, but it appears in many forms. As a representative of hedonism, Epicurus was preceded by Aristippus, a student of Socrates, and by his Cyrenaic school. However, the hedonism of Epicurus is far subtler and more noble than that of Aristippus and many others. For Epicurus philosophy means the art of living and a kind of medicine that leads man to a healthy and, therefore, happy life.[30] According to the third epistle of Epicurus, philosophy is to be practiced by both young and old, since the health of the soul and happiness can and should be obtained in every moment of life. The young become happier when they free themselves from the fear of the future, and the old are happy when they enjoy the memory of past pleasures and good deeds.[31] The knowledge of physics presenting to us a universe moved by natural causes and divine beings unconcerned with our affairs serves to free us from fear, and that is its principal function.[32] Even the fear of death is eliminated, for according to the famous saying of Epicurus, when we are, death is not, and when death is, we are not.[33] We must free ourselves from the desire for a future and eternal

---

30. Usener, fr. 219–221, 297; Arrighetti, fr. 230, 347.
31. *Epist.* 3.122; *Gnom. Vat.* 7 (ed. von der Muehll).
32. *Epist.* 1.82; 2.85; and *Sententiae* 2.
33. *Epist.* 3.125. See *Sententiae* 2.

life. The wise man enjoys the most pleasurable moment, but not the longest time, and the length of time adds nothing to the pleasure of the present moment.[34] Pleasure and happiness consist, therefore, in the present and actual experience and are not increased by the extension of time. This explains the accent on the present that sounds in the *Carpe diem* of Horace and in the *Laetus in praesens* of Ficino. On the other hand, there is no sense in trusting a future that is not within our power. The man who looks to the future is losing the present, and he who is less dependent on the future reaches it more pleasurably.

Epicurus' theory of the passions (*epithumiai*) clearly illustrates how removed his hedonism is from the vulgar hedonism with which it has often, and dishonestly, been confused by his adversaries. Our desires are partly natural and partly empty, and of those that are natural some are necessary and some are not.[35] We should satisfy desires that are natural and necessary, not those which are empty. Of the natural but not necessary desires, only those having otherwise negative consequences should be satisfied.[36] Desires for food and for clothing are necessary, and sexual desire is natural, but not necessary. Desires for particular foods, particular clothes, or particular sexual acts are neither natural nor necessary, but empty.[37] Desires that are natural and necessary are easy, empty desires are difficult to fulfill. Hence, we make our life happier if we limit our desires to the necessary ones that can be easily satis-

34. *Epist.* 3.125; *Sententiae* 19; *Gnom. Vat.* 14; Usener, fr. 490, 491; Arrighetti, fr. 242, 245.

35. *Epist.* 3.127.

36. *Gnom. Vat.* 21 and 71.

37. Usener, fr. 456.

fied. True wealth consists in being self-sufficient.[38] With regard to sexual desires, Epicurus is more ascetic than many other philosophers and advises the wise man to avoid love, considering that its consequences are never useful, and often harmful.[39]

The end of our life in which our happiness consists (and according to which we must regulate our actions and what we must choose and avoid) is the health of the body and the tranquillity of the soul (*ataraxia*). We must avoid at all costs what brings pain to the body or disquiet to the soul. Therefore, our happiness does not depend on wealth or power, but on the health of the body and on the tranquillity of the soul, which limits itself to what is natural.[40] True pleasure really consists in the absence of pain, and we need pleasure only when its absence brings us pain. When we do not feel pain, we do not need pleasure.[41] It is for these reasons and in this sense that we consider pleasure as the principle and end of the happy life and as the criterion according to which we should make our choices.[42] Even the animals follow the same criterion—that is, they choose pleasure and avoid pain.[43] But neither do we choose all pleasures, nor avoid all pain, without distinction. We avoid many pleasures because they are followed by greater pain, and we choose many painful things because they lead us to greater pleasure. Every choice and every action must be judged according to its useful or harmful

38. *Epist.* 3.130–31; *Sententiae* 15 and 26; Usener, fr. 454ff., 469, 473, 476; Arrighetti, fr. 240, 218.

39. *Gnom. Vat.* 51; Usener, fr. 483, 574.

40. *Epist.*, 3, 128. See Usener, fr. 2, 548; Arrighetti, fr. 7, 144.

41. *Epist.* 2.128; Usener, fr. 417, 422; Arrighetti, fr. 197.

42. *Epist.* 3.129.

43. Usener, fr. 397, 398.

consequences. Instead of choosing any pleasure without regard to its consequences, we must calculate the pleasures and
pains connected with a particular action:[44] "When we say that
pleasure constitutes the end, we do not mean the pleasures of
the unbridled . . . as those who do not know us or do not
agree with us or misunderstand us believe, but what we mean
is simply the absence of pain in the body and of disquiet in
the soul. It is not the pleasures of the senses that make life
pleasurable, rather it is sober reasoning that examines the
causes of every positive or negative choice and eliminates all
those opinions that most things that trouble our souls are
based on."[45] It is such sentences as these that have led even
some followers of rival schools, like Seneca, to defend Epicurus against the exaggerated attacks of his adversaries.[46]

The theory of the virtues, which holds a central place in
many ethical systems, is not neglected by Epicurus, but he
makes the point that virtues are bound together and, in a
certain sense, subordinate to pleasure: "It is not possible to
live pleasurably without prudence or virtue or justice," and
"virtues are bound together [*sumpephukasi*] with the pleasurable life."[47] But he adds that we must honor the good and the
virtues and other things of the kind only if they lead to pleasure. If not, we must let them go.[48] We must especially avoid
those virtues that are empty and vain and that lead to disquiet-
ing hopes.[49] We must choose the virtues not for themselves,
but for the pleasure they bring us, as we choose a medication

44. *Epist.* 3.129–30; Usener, fr. 442; Arrighetti, fr. 129.

45. *Epist.* 3.131–32; *Sententiae* 10.

46. Usener, fr. 460.

47. *Epist.* 3.132; *Sententiae* 5.

48. Usener, fr. 70; Arrighetti, fr. 22, 4.

49. Usener, fr. 116; Arrighetti, fr. 42.

for the good health that follows it.[50] On the other hand, virtue is inseparable from pleasure, and without pleasure there is no virtue.[51] But virtue is not enough for the happy life, just as happiness is not solely based on virtue, but on the pleasure that follows from virtue.[52] Epicurus disdains the kind of virtue that is empty and is not followed by pleasure,[53] that is, virtue as it was conceived by his Stoic rivals.

With regard to pain and other physical ills, the Epicurean philosopher bears them with strength, and on this point he is no different from his Stoic contemporaries. Illness and pain have either a limited power or a short length.[54] Great suffering will soon kill us, and the illnesses which last longer are less serious.[55] The evils and the goods of fortune have no importance for the life of the wise man. The good and evil that concern the common lot last but a while, and the wisdom of the philosopher does not depend on fortune.[56] The wise man is always happy, even when he is tormented, even when he is roasting inside the bull of Phalaris.[57] Reading these passages without knowing their author, no one would think of Epicurus, and that stems from the popular and erroneous opinion held of his philosophy.

In his scattered remarks, Epicurus also offers a theory of law and justice that is interesting and different from the better-known ones of Aristotle and the Stoics. We might call his

---

50. Usener, fr. 504.

51. Usener, fr. 506.

52. Usener, fr. 508.

53. Usener, fr. 512; Arrighetti, fr. 136.

54. *Epist.* 3.133; *Sententiae* 4; *Gnom. Vat.* 4.

55. Usener, fr. 447; Arrighetti, fr. 204.

56. *Epist.* 3.134–35; Usener, fr. 489, 584; Arrighetti, fr. 210.

57. Usener, fr. 601.

theory "naturalistic." Justice for him is based on a contract consisting of a mutual promise by the parties not to harm one another.[58] When there are no such contracts, one cannot speak of justice or injustice—hence, the concept of law or justice does not apply to animals or to certain primitive and savage tribes.[59] The just is what is useful and it is the same for everyone, but it varies according to regions and peoples, and even according to the times.[60] This theory of the just as a contract is connected with the general principles of Epicurean ethics. The just man is free from all disquiet, and the unjust man is full of troubles.[61] Injustice is an evil not so much for itself, but for the fear that comes with it, since the wrongdoer never knows whether sooner or later his crime will be discovered.[62]

According to Epicurus, no man chooses evil as such, but is deceived by some good aspect which tempts him, and then he falls prey to a greater and unforeseen evil.[63] The wise man will avoid not only love but also family life, and even political life.[64] He seeks out a hidden life (*lathe biosas*)[65] and avoids all publicity. On the other hand, he does not lead the solitary life of a hermit, but participates in a shared existence based on friendship, living in his school together with his fellow philosophers. Epicurus gives great importance to the friendship that binds the teacher to his disciples and the disciples to each

58. *Sententiae* 31.
59. *Sententiae* 32.
60. *Sententiae* 36–38.
61. *Sententiae* 17.
62. *Sententiae* 35.
63. *Gnom. Vat.* 16.
64. Usener, fr. 19, 523–525.
65. Usener, fr. 551.

other: "Among the treasures that wisdom contributes to life, the greatest is the gift of friendship."[66] Characteristically Epicurean is the entirely personal way that the teacher must serve as a model for the life of his disciples and followers. The life of Epicurus, his kindness and self-sufficiency, must be our model.[67] We should always live as if Epicurus were watching us.[68] Contrary to his Stoic rivals, Epicurus permits the philosopher to feel sorrow at the death of a friend, insisting that the absence of sorrow in this case comes from another evil, heartlessness,[69] and pointing to the pleasure in consolation that comes with our tears in such a situation. We are reminded as well of the pleasure that accompanies the memory of past joys in an elderly wise man.[70]

The humane spirit of the philosophy of Epicurus is movingly expressed in the brief letter written by him shortly before his death. "We are writing you this letter as we pass on and end this blessed day of our life. My pains in the bladder and the intestines continue with great force and do not let up. But set against them all is my soul's delight at the memory of our past conversations. Show yourself worthy of the regard you have had since your youth for me and for philosophy. And take care of the sons of Metrodorus."[71]

The center and goal of the philosophy of Epicurus is the tranquillity and serenity of the soul, which is the product of a

66. *Sententiae* 27.

67. *Gnom. Vat.* 36.

68. Usener, fr. 211; Arrighetti, fr. 223.

69. Usener, fr. 120; Arrighetti, fr. 46.

70. Usener, fr. 186.

71. Usener, fr. 138; Arrighetti, fr. 52. For the humane spirit of Epicurus, we should also read his testament and his letter to a child: Usener, fr. 176, 217; Arrighetti, fr. 261, 13–17 (Diog. Laert. 10.16–21).

concrete moral experience that is renewed and repeated every day in the midst of the vicissitudes of life. All the philosophical doctrines of Epicurus, including his epistemology and physics, are subordinate to this end. His letters and sentences are meant to serve as moral instructions in certain concrete and particular situations, and not simply as general rules for moral life. Epicurus was trying to realize in everyday life his own moral ideal, and to his friends and disciples he offered himself as a model, a guide, and a liberator. This explains the wealth of personal details that have been preserved about him, as well as the lasting impression he made not only on his followers but on those of his readers not taken in by the prejudices of his adversaries. We may well not agree with his doctrines (and I am quite far from sharing the majority of his teachings), but we must consider Epicurus as one of the wisest and most humane of the moralists of classical antiquity. His influence was not limited to his school, which continued and flourished for many centuries and upheld his doctrine with notable fidelity.

Epicurean doctrine, at least in some of its facets, was acceptable even among such Stoic thinkers as Chrysippus and Seneca, and with such neo-Platonists as Plotinus and Porphyry, thinkers who in the general outlines of their thought were rather alien to Epicureanism. We have also seen how some of the themes of Epicurus' thought were taken up and modified by many philosophers and scientists between the fifteenth and seventeenth centuries, and the traces of this influence may also be found in more modern and even in contemporary thought. The analysis of these influences always leads to complex results, since thinkers who follow the ideas of a predecessor never repeat them mechanically, but cast them in their own new way of thinking, which includes many ideas that are both either original or of different origins. It is always important to recognize in thinkers what they have borrowed from their predecessors and not to consider as original to them ideas that are in fact quotations from classical sources or from other thinkers. I know of many examples of this in the interpretations of humanism and of the Renaissance, and I will readily admit that I myself have sometimes committed similar errors. The alleged originality of a thinker often reflects the ignorance of his readers and interpreters. Nonetheless, I have always insisted that the quotations and borrowings of a later thinker must be interpreted in the context of his whole thought, which includes many different and original elements. I would gladly say: "That goes without saying," and I can see no justification for the pretentious theories that are now in vogue which speak of intertextuality (we might with equal right speak of "interconceptuality" when speaking of concepts rather than texts). Such theories often do nothing but add an artificial and obscure terminology to facts that are well known and understood through the help of the "traditional" method of the historical and philological sciences. When this method is ignored, modern theorizations lead to arbitrary or mistaken interpretations of our texts, which I might call "extratextuality" rather than intertextuality. In any case, the thought of Epicurus and of his school offers us an example of the contribution that Hellenistic thought has made and continues to make to the Western philosophical tradition.

I might have begun these lectures with Zeno rather than with Epicurus, since they were almost contemporaries. But I decided to begin with Epicurus because his school constitutes in a certain sense a separate branch of ancient philosophy which had little influence on the other schools and which took little from them in the way of influences and, therefore, is suited to an independent treatment. On the other hand, the Stoic and Academic schools underwent a continuous development characterized by reciprocal influences between the two and by continual modifications due to these influences. So we shall try to deal with these two schools in the chronological sequence of their transformations and not interrupt them with a description of Epicureanism, a different system that called for a separate treatment.

CHAPTER TWO

Zeno and Cleanthes

Zeno, the founder of the Stoic school, was a contemporary of
Epicurus, and his school was for many centuries the principal
rival of the school of Epicurus. Stoic doctrine, as distinct and
often opposed to Epicurean doctrine as it was, still had some
elements similar to it and even in common with it. The Stoic
theory of knowledge was also radically empiricist and its physics purely materialist, and in the Stoic system as well epistemology and physics were subordinate to ethics, which was
the central element of its teaching. But whereas in the Epicurean school the authentic doctrine of the founder and teacher
was kept almost intact down to the end of classical Antiquity,
Stoic doctrine was greatly enriched and even modified by

Zeno's successors over the course of the centuries. In contrast to Epicurus, not many of the original texts or fragments of Zeno have come down to us—hence we cannot always say whether the teachings attributed to his successors, and especially to Chrysippus, stem from Zeno. Following the example of Arnim and other scholars, we will stick to the teachings explicitly attributed by the subsequent tradition to Zeno and ascribe many other Stoic teachings to Chrysippus and his successors.

The influence of Stoicism and especially of Stoic ethics has indeed been very far-reaching and long-lasting. We find it in many Roman thinkers and also jurists, in Middle Platonism and in neo-Platonism, in Philo and in many Fathers of the Church, in medieval philosophy and among the humanists. In the sixteenth century and after, there was even a rebirth of Stoicism represented by Pomponazzi, Justus Lipsius, and others. Among the philosophers of the modern age, we find strong elements of Stoicism in the ethics of Spinoza, of Kant, and others. Nietzsche himself—despite his opposition to the philosophy of Plato and other ancient thinkers, and notwithstanding his prejudice in favor of the pre-Socratics, who represent for him the heroic age of classical thought—follows Stoic teaching on some essential points, although he does not admit to it. Indeed, both his doctrine of fate and of the eternal return are clearly Stoic. Moreover, Stoicism too, though less so than Epicureanism, has been misunderstood and falsified by its adversaries, often in bad faith, so that, as with all philosophers of the past, many erroneous opinions about it, however widespread, remain to be corrected.

Zeno of Citium, a native of Cyprus, came to Athens after 320 B.C. He was influenced by Xenocrates and other members of the Old Academy of Plato, as well as by the school of the Cynics Antisthenes and Diogenes. He began to teach around 300 B.C. in the *Stoa Poikile*, which gave its name to his school, and he died circa 264. He was highly respected and even publicly honored for the austerity of his character and his simplicity of life. But he was also criticized for his new terminology, a criticism that has been leveled at all philosophers down to our own day (and I myself criticize many contemporary philosophers for this), but which is only partially justified. A concept that is valid, but new, has always led to the creation of new technical terms, and the history of philosophical and scientific thought is reflected in the history of terminology, which is an indispensable key for understanding the thought of the past and of the present. A new terminology deserves to be criticized only when it reflects empty and erroneous concepts, or when it serves as a pretext for repeating in artificial or obscure language the same ideas that can be expressed in simple and clear language. In Zeno's case, as in the case of many other serious thinkers, we are inclined to grant him the right to change his terminology in order to express his thought with greater precision.

Zeno, after Xenocrates, divides philosophy into three parts: logic, physics, and ethics.[1] In his theory of knowledge he makes a fundamental distinction between sure knowledge and mere opinion (*doxa*), and he holds that the sage must not affirm any opinion that has no basis in sure knowledge.[2] This distinction, which reflects Plato's distinction between knowledge and opinion, is the basis of Stoic dogmatism. But for Zeno, unlike Plato, the basis of all our knowledge is perception and, more precisely, comprehending representation (*phantasia kataleptike*).[3] This representation which grasps its ob-

---

1. Arnim 1, fr. 45, 46. (All references to Arnim in this chapter are to H. von Arnim, *Stoicorum Veterum Fragmenta*, 4 vols.)

2. Arnim 1, fr. 52–54.

3. Arnim 1, fr. 56.

ject is impressed and sealed on our soul on the basis of an existing object[4] and corresponds to this existing object in a manner that could not be produced by a nonexistent object.[5] The term "comprehension" (*katalepsis*) was coined by Zeno to indicate that our representation, when valid, directly grasps its object,[6] and our current usage, which makes us grasp or comprehend a thing, still reflects this Stoic doctrine and terminology. Also important is the distinction Zeno makes between what exists and what does not exist and the relationship they have, according to him, with our thought.[7] The concept, later to be developed by Chrysippus, reflects a clearly nominalist point of view, which distinguishes sharply between the object that exists outside our thought and our perception which refers to it. For Plato, and for Aristotle as well, our concepts are direct reflections of an objective reality that, according to Plato, is separate from particular objects and, according to Aristotle, is inherent in them, but for them there is no need to assume a real existence prior to and independent of the knowledge we have of them. The term "to exist" (*huparkhein*) and the derivative term describing the "existing object" (*to huparkhon*), while already in use in ordinary language, acquire for Zeno and his successors a technical meaning previously unknown. Indeed, I am convinced that the abstract term "existence" (*huparxis*), which derives from it, is also of Stoic origin, even though it is not to be found in the fragments of Zeno and his successors, but only in later authors.[8] The word, and the

4. Arnim 1, fr. 58.

5. Arnim 1, fr. 59.

6. Arnim 1, fr. 60.

7. Arnim 1, fr. 59.

8. The substantive *huparxis* does not appear in Arnim's index (4:149). The *Thesaurus Linguae Graecae* (computerized printout), ed. Theodore

concept it reflects, is not found in Plato or Aristotle (and we have tried to indicate why). The concept of existence, which became so important from the fourteenth century on, had its origins not, as has been suggested, in some texts of Aristotle or the Bible, but clearly derives from neo-Platonic sources and perhaps in the last analysis from Stoic sources.[9]

F. Brunner et al., notes its presence in Zeno (fr. 113, from Sextus Empiricus) and in Chrysippus (2, fr. 153, from Galen; fr. 223, from Sextus; fr. 337, from Sextus; fr. 356, from Galen; fr. 404, from Sextus; fr. 536, from Alexander of Aphrodisias; fr. 1016, from Sextus; and 3, fr. 466, from Galen), but all these passages are paraphrases, and we are not sure that the use of the term is original. In *A Greek-English Lexicon*, ed. Liddell, Scott, and Jones (Oxford: Oxford University Press, 1966), the noun *huparxis* is attested for Philodemus, Plutarch, Plotinus, and many later authors (in the *Thesaurus* also for Philo of Alexandria and many later authors). It is also found in a fragment of Gorgias' *Die Fragmente der Vorsokratiker*, ed. and trans. H. Diels and W. Kranz, 11th ed. (Zurich and Berlin: Weidmann, 1964), vol. 2, pp. 279–83, no. 82, Gorgias B 3, from Sextus Empiricus, *Adversus mathematicos* 7:65–87 (at 7.71).

9. *Existentia* as the translation of *huparxis* appears many times in Robert Grosseteste's translation of Pseudo-Dionysius the Areopagite, *Dionysiaca* (Paris: Desclée de Brouwer, 1937), pp. 41, 73, 76, 84, 146, 147, 186, 267, 332, 755, 1109, 1199, 1365, and 1414. It also appears in William of Moerbeke's translation of the *Elementatio Theologica* of Proclus in C. Vansteenkiste, ed., *Tijdschrift voor Philosophie*, vol. 13 (1951), pp. 263–302, 491–531, and vol. 14 (1952), pp. 503–46; see also *Propositiones* 9, 24, 64, 65, 67, 86, 118, 120–122, 133, 140, 141, 153, 166, 173, and 192; and also in William of Moerbeke's translation of Proclus' *Tria Opuscula*, ed. H. Boese (Berlin: W. de Gruyter, 1960), p. 294. See H. Boese, "Wilhelm von Moerbeke als Übersetzer der Stoicheiosis theologike des Proclus," *Abhandlungen der Heidelberger Akademie der*

The distinction made by Zeno between comprehending and uncomprehending representations indicates that for him (unlike Epicurus), not every perception is true and valid, and that we must distinguish between valid and invalid perceptions, and accept only valid perceptions.[10] This distinction leads Zeno to an innovation with respect to Aristotelian logic, one that had great influence on subsequent thought but which has not been clearly understood or appreciated. Since our perception may derive from either existing or nonexistent objects, and only the perception that comes from an existing object may be accepted as valid, we must add our assent (*sunkatathesis*) to every received perception, and this assent represents our rational and voluntary judgment.[11] Perception itself is not valid without this assent, and comprehending perceptions are precisely those that elicit our assent.

The notions of general substances and qualities are also representations in our soul, and their objects are nonexistent. The ideas of Plato are nothing but notions (*ennoiai*) of our soul.[12] Zeno and his successors, therefore, reduce Platonic ideas to mere notions and follow on this point, as on some others, the doctrine of Antisthenes, who had denied the objective existence of ideas and had reduced them to simple notions of our soul.[13]

Wissenschaften, Philosophisch-Historische Klasse (Jahrgang 1985), no. 5; P. O. Kristeller, "Proclus as a Reader of Plato and Plotinus and His Influence in the Middle Ages and in the Renaissance," in *Proclus: Lecteur et interprète des Anciens*, ed. J. Pépin and H. D. Saffrey (Paris: CNRS,1987), pp. 191–211 (at p. 205).

10. Arnim 1, fr. 60.

11. Arnim 1, fr. 61.

12. Arnim 1, fr. 65.

13. *Socraticorum Reliquiae*, ed. G. Giannantoni, vol. 2, p. 375 (Antis-

In his physics Zeno distinguishes two fundamental principles: God, who is material, but active, and matter, which is
passive.[14] Zeno further asserts that there is only one world,
which is finite, but surrounded by an infinite void.[15] There is
no void inside the world,[16] and to avoid the possibility that
the mixing of various bodies might produce an internal void,
Zeno introduces the concept of a total mixture in which every
element penetrates the other completely without leaving any
interval so that even the smallest particle of the mixed body
contains elements of all its ingredients.[17] Among the four elements Zeno, following Heraclitus, gives special importance to
fire.[18] He distinguishes two types of fire—the ordinary fire
that destroys all other bodies, which he calls artless fire (*pur
atekhnon*), and the more subtle fire, which he calls artificial fire
(*pur tekhnikon*)[19] and which he identifies with a material but
subtle substance that penetrates everything and that he calls
spirit (*pneuma*). This spirit or artificial fire constitutes the substance of God and of all of nature and also of the rational soul,
so that God and the soul are corporeal and material. Echoing
Plato and Aristotle, Zeno treats the physical world and even
the celestial spheres as animals governed by rational souls.[20]
God contains in himself the seeds of all the parts of the world,

---

thenes, section 5A), fr. 149 (Simplicius, in *Categorias* 208.28–32; Ammonius, in *Isagogem* 40.6–10; and Tzetzes, *Chiliad.* 7.605–609). See
also Diogenes Laertius, *Vitae et Placita philosophorum* 6.53.

14. Arnim 1, fr. 85.
15. Arnim 1. fr. 95, 97.
16. Arnim 1, fr. 95.
17. Arnim 1, fr. 92.
18. Arnim 1, fr. 98.
19. Arnim 1. fr. 120.
20. Arnim 1, fr. 135, 138, 142, 154, 157.

and the soul contains the seeds of all the parts of the body. Hence, God is called the seminal reason (*spermatikos logos*) of the world,[21] and the soul is like the seminal reason of the body. Here we have the origin of a concept and a terminology developed by Chrysippus and taken up first by the neo-Platonists and then by St. Augustine, to whom this concept is often attributed as an original contribution by historians who have no knowledge of Hellenistic philosophy.

The world has four levels, which correspond to rational beings, to animals, to plants, and to inanimate beings like minerals.[22] The soul has eight parts—that is, the principal part (*hegemonikon*), the part capable of speech (*phonetikon*), the five senses (in common with the animals), and the generative or vegetative part (in common also with plants).[23] Minerals do not possess a soul but have a quality called coherence (*hexis*), which holds every being together and separates it from others.[24] God is present on all these levels but is active primarily as the reason (*logos*) of the world.[25]

God as a subtle fire penetrates the whole world and acts as the soul of the world and as providence.[26] He is identical with the natural and divine law that governs everything and also operates as irresistible fate (*heimarmene*).[27] The Stoic system teaches a determinism that is very rigid and certainly more radical than that of all the other ancient schools. This determinism includes a doctrine of the eternal cycle. After well-

21. Arnim 1, fr. 102 (p. 28, line 26, from Diog. Laert. 7.136).
22. Arnim 1, fr. 158.
23. Arnim 1, fr. 143.
24. Arnim 1, fr. 158.
25. Ibid.
26. Arnim 1, fr. 153, 172.
27. Arnim 1, fr. 160, 176.

determined periodic intervals the entire world is destroyed by fire and then remade, and every new world repeats exactly and in all its particulars the preceding world, so that all the people and all the events of the past return an infinite number of times.[28]

Stoicism like the other ancient schools of philosophy has its own theology, but it seeks to justify the popular religion of the Greeks with allegorical interpretations,[29] following a method used already by the sophists and other ancient thinkers and later applied to the Bible by Jewish and Christian theologians since the time of Philo of Alexandria.

Zeno's ethics is based on his definition of the moral end. The end consists in living in accord with nature, which is the same as living according to virtue.[30] This definition demonstrates by itself the close bond between the ethical and physical doctrine of the Stoics. Zeno also insists that virtue is sufficient for happiness.[31] Nothing is good outside of virtue and of what participates in virtue, and nothing is bad but vice and what participates in vice.[32] All the other things that are popularly considered good or bad, like life and death, fame and infamy, pain and pleasure, wealth and poverty, health and sickness, are morally indifferent (_adiaphora_).[33] However, among the things indifferent one must distinguish between what is preferable (_proegmena_) and what is not preferable (_apoproegmena_), according to a distinction and a terminology introduced

28. Arnim 1, fr. 107, 109.
29. Arnim 1, fr. 167–170.
30. Arnim 1, fr. 179.
31. Arnim 1, fr. 187.
32. Arnim 1, fr. 190.
33. Ibid.

by Zeno.[34] Preferable things do not contribute directly to happiness, but are preferable just the same and with a certain degree of necessity.[35] Thus it happens that Stoic ethics, in theory the most rigid and severe of all, in practice may become rather opportunistic since in the vast territory of things intermediate between virtue and vice philosophers feel free to choose things indifferent, but preferable, and so to follow the course most advantageous to themselves.

Virtue and vice are attributes of the dominant parts of our soul,[36] and the ethical status of this part is the basis of all our particular actions.[37] Therefore, all virtues are inseparable one from the other and we have them all or we have none.[38] So ethics is based on a single principle and on a single moral status upon which all particular actions depend and on the basis of which all particular cases are decided. Here we find ourselves at the opposite pole of the widespread tendency in the moral philosophy of our times which tries to treat each particular case by itself without recourse to a universal ethical principle, in the belief that general principles either do not exist at all or that they may be defined only on the basis of many particular cases, and that the moral quality of a particular case may be established on the basis of an individual or collective *feeling* (a position that strikes me as not only contrary to philosophical tradition but as quite absurd in and of itself).

Differently from Aristotle, but in agreement with Epicurus, Zeno treats the theory of the passions as an essential part of

34. Arnim 1, fr. 192.
35. Ibid.
36. Arnim 1, fr. 202.
37. Arnim 1, fr. 203.
38. Arnim 1, fr. 199, 200.

ethics. Indeed, his theory of the passions is more rigid and more systematic than that of the other ancient philosophers. Passion is defined as an excessive impulse or as an irrational and unnatural movement of the soul.[39] Zeno distinguishes four principal kinds of passions: pain, fear, pleasure, and desire.[40] This scheme dominated the philosophical tradition until the seventeenth century and is still traceable in the theories of Descartes and Leibniz. Zeno goes on to define the particular passions (beginning with pain) as a form of opinion.[41] He points out that the passions are not only emotional impulses but are also irrational and mistaken judgments that may be corrected by more rational judgments. Indeed, the purpose of ethical discourse is to overcome the passions and even to root them out, not simply to moderate them, as Aristotle and his followers had taught.[42] Stoic moral teaching is extremely intellectualistic and rejects all emotions and all sentiments as irrational. On this point Zeno is following the position of Socrates and ignores the Aristotelian doctrine of incontinence, in which Aristotle criticizes and modifies the rationalism of Socrates by saying that knowledge alone is not enough to restrain our passions. This passage in Aristotle has been much discussed by recent scholars, who tend to exaggerate his position in favor of an extreme irrationalism dear to them but not shared by the philosopher.

Rejecting all the emotions and all the sentiments as ethical factors, Zeno also eliminates compassion and mercy as ethical motives because they are based on sentiment and not on rea-

39. Arnim 1, fr. 205.
40. Arnim 1, fr. 211.
41. Arnim 1, fr. 212.
42. Arnim 1, fr. 207.

son.[43] On this point the Stoics were criticized by Christian thinkers for whom compassion, often praised in the Bible, held an important ethical value. Certain contemporary thinkers who base their own ethical doctrines on compassion do not seem to realize that they are reviving religious and Christian motives and take a stand against the rationalistic tradition that goes from the Stoics to Kant, which is based on other principles and deals with other ethical problems that cannot be reduced to compassion.

Typically Stoic is the radical distinction between wise men (*sophoi* or *spoudaioi*) and foolish or bad men (*phauloi*). According to Zeno, the wise follow and practice the virtues through their whole lives, and the foolish always follow the vices. The sage possesses by definition all the good qualities. He is great and strong, happy and pious, a good king and a good citizen, whereas the fool has all the opposite qualities.[44] Going beyond this level of reasoning, we arrive at the so-called Stoic paradoxes. The sage is always free, even when he is a slave; rich, even when a beggar; beautiful, even when he is ugly.[45] These are postulates in which the qualities are understood in a higher sense and the common understanding of the same qualities has no importance. All wise men are friends of each other, even if they do not know each other, and all the fools are enemies of each other.[46] The Stoic paradoxes have often been discussed by later writers, even with reference to nobility, a theme dear to the humanists and their successors. For example, the concept of nobility as the consequence of virtue as

43. Arnim 1, fr. 213, 214.
44. Arnim 1, fr. 216.
45. Arnim 1, fr. 218–221.
46. Arnim 1, fr. 223, 226.

defended in the dialogues of Buonaccorso da Montemagno and Poggio Bracciolini is clearly derived from the Stoic paradoxes known to them from Cicero and other authors. If we do not take these paradoxes too literally, they show an attitude that makes man freer from his external circumstances and more or less self-sufficient and autonomous in his interior disposition.

Zeno also coined a term that was to have a long and complex history. He speaks of what is proper and pertinent in a moral sense (*kathekon*) and explains it as belonging to certain people and certain situations. He also defines it as what, when put into practice, has a plausible justification.[47] According to Zeno this attribute is applicable also to animals,[48] and he does not consider it as good, but as intermediary between good and evil and apparently as preferable.[49] We shall see later that this concept assumed a central importance in the thought of Panaetius and then had a lasting influence on Western thought from Cicero to Kant. Ironically, and as the consequence of two inexact translations (*officium* in Latin and *duty* in the modern languages), this has become a central concept in many modern discussions on ethics, replacing the highest good—happiness and virtue.

Finally, Zeno formulated the concept and the ideal of cosmopolitanism. Since there is only one world, we must believe that all human beings are citizens of this world.[50] This ideal is

47. Arnim 1, fr. 230.

48. Ibid.

49. Arnim 1, fr. 231–232.

50. Arnim 1, fr. 262. See Diogenes of Sinope, who says that the only true republic existing is the world. *Socraticorum Reliquiae*, ed. G. Giannantoni, vol. 2, p. 548 (Diogenes Sinopeus, section 5B), fr. 353, lines 14–15 (Diog. Laert. 6.72).

contrary to all the ancient and modern particularisms and nationalisms, but it has had wide appeal in many ages, and also in our century. It has often been forgotten that the merit of this concept is due to Zeno, but this should be recalled in order to remind us that the treasury of ancient philosophy contains many ideas that are not only still valid but ought to be appreciated and reevaluated in the present, and perhaps in the future.

Zeno had many immediate disciples who partly modified his doctrine, like Ariston of Chios and Herillus of Carthage. Better known is Cleanthes of Assos, who succeeded Zeno as the head of the school. We should also speak briefly of him, since he added some interesting aspects to Zeno's doctrine. Cleanthes lived from 330 to 231 B.C. and from 264 until his death he was the head of the Stoa.

Cleanthes distinguishes six parts of philosophy, subdividing each of the conventional three parts into two: dialectic and rhetoric, ethics and politics, physics and theology.[51] It seems he primarily developed the physics of Zeno and gave special significance to theology. A hymn to Zeus by Cleanthes has been preserved, which is the longest and most impressive of the texts we have from the ancient Stoics.[52] Not by chance, Cleanthes holds that the meter and rhythm of poetry are closer to the truth of theology than the discursive prose of the philosophers.[53] He repeats that universal ideas are simple notions[54] and that the world soul fills the whole universe, and he explicitly adds that the human soul is a part of the world soul.[55] In

51. Arnim 1, fr. 482.
52. Arnim 1, fr. 357 (preserved by Stobaeus).
53. Arnim 1, fr. 486.
54. Arnim 1, fr. 494.
55. Arnim 1, fr. 495.

some other verses, preserved by Epictetus and translated by Seneca, Cleanthes states that he will go without fear where God and fate lead him and that, if he becomes evil, he will have to do so even without wanting to.[56] This is a first attempt to face the problem implicit in Zeno's doctrine—that is, how to reconcile universal determinism with the freedom of the wise man, a problem also addressed by Chrysippus. Cleanthes attempts to explain the origin of the notions of the gods in the human soul.[57] He affirms that the existence of God as a being more perfect than man is necessary,[58] and he identifies Zeus or God with the world soul.[59] To this supreme God he addresses the verses of his famous hymn. God governs all with his law, but only men among the creatures of the earth are close to him. Nothing in the world happens without God apart from the irrational acts of evil men. God brings things that are discordant to a universal concord, that is, to a universal Logos which unites all contrasts. Good men obey with reason the common law of God and lead a good life, while bad men devoid of reason flee this law and fall from one evil to another. The hymn closes with the prayer that Zeus free all men from their folly and teach them to honor his empire and to praise his law and his rule of the world.[60]

In his ethical teaching Cleanthes follows Zeno and repeats that happiness consists in harmony with nature, but he adds that one must be in harmony with universal nature rather than with a particular nature, thus giving the ethical prin-

56. Arnim 1, fr. 527.
57. Arnim 1, fr. 528.
58. Arnim 1, fr. 529.
59. Arnim 1, fr. 532.
60. Arnim 1, fr. 537.

ciple of Zeno a cosmological and theological significance.[61] Cleanthes insists that all men have by nature a disposition (*aphorme*) toward virtue and that the foolish leave this disposition in an imperfect condition, whereas the wise perfect it.[62] In this way the rigid dualism between the foolish and the wise set down by Zeno is mitigated, and the way is opened for the possible passage from one status to the other, a concept later developed by Panaetius. Cleanthes insists in agreement with Zeno that virtue may be taught[63] and that once it has been attained it cannot be lost, since it is based on solid knowledge.[64] Pleasure has no value and is not a natural end.[65] The sage has no need of it, since nothing is bad except vice.[66]

Ancient Stoicism as formulated by Zeno and slightly modified by Cleanthes constitutes one of the most precise and influential classical models in the history of ethics and of all of philosophy. Its theory of knowledge is different from that of Epicurus, but no less empirical. Its physics is materialist like that of Epicurus, but determinist as well, and does not offer a physical system comparable in force and coherence to the atomism of Democritus and of Epicurus. Stoic ethics, with its doctrine of things indifferent but preferable, opens to its followers the road toward an active and political life limited and controlled by precise ethical principles, whereas the Epicurean wise man, with few exceptions, keeps far away from political

61. Arnim 1, fr. 555.
62. Arnim 1, fr. 566.
63. Arnim 1, fr. 567.
64. Arnim 1, fr. 568.
65. Arnim 1, fr. 574.
66. Arnim 1, fr. 577.

life. Therefore, it is not surprising to find among the Roman statesmen many Stoic philosophers like Cato the Younger, Seneca, and Marcus Aurelius.

An important contribution of the Stoics to ethical, political, and legal thought, later developed by Chrysippus, was the concept and the doctrine of natural law, which has had an enormous influence down to recent times. This doctrine has been confused in many recent discussions by several misunderstandings regarding its historical origins, its content, and its intrinsic value. One often reads that natural law comes from Aristotle, but this confuses two different doctrines. Aristotle is referring to the discussions of the sophists, well known to Plato, according to which law and justice are based on convention and not on nature (a position favored by the Greek term *nomos*, meaning both law and convention). Aristotle, agreeing with Socrates and Plato, affirms that justice is based on nature, and not on convention. This theory is important and, I find, valid, but has nothing to do with natural law, which is a distinctly Stoic concept based on Stoic cosmology. The Stoics identify their God and the world soul with a law (*nomos*) that governs the whole world and thus is both divine and natural.[67] They add that all human laws follow the model of universal law and derive their validity from their agreement with this natural law. In other words, human law can be bad when it does not agree with the universal law, and we assume that our reason can comprehend the universal law and judge every human law according to its agreement or disagreement with that natural law. This concept was taken over and transformed by St. Augustine, who identifies the divine law with a neo-Platonic idea contained in the mind of God and the natural law with an innate idea in the human mind that is a copy

67. Arnim 1, fr. 162.

of the divine idea.[68] This concept passed from St. Augustine to many medieval thinkers including St. Thomas, and so this doctrine has also become part of modern Catholic thought. But it is mistaken to think that the doctrine is exclusively or prevalently Catholic, as is sometimes said. Its origin is Stoic, not Aristotelian, and, to a certain point, neo-Platonic. The Stoic doctrine was then passed down through Cicero and other jurists to the *Corpus Iuris* of Justinian (which preserves the original Greek text of the first words of the treatise of Chrysippus on law)[69] and was, therefore, discussed and defended in the Middle Ages not only by philosophers and theologians but also by jurists.

We also find the concept of natural law in the thought of many authors of the Early Modern period who have nothing to do with Catholic theology, like Hugo Grotius and Spinoza.[70] The concept is even implicit in the thought of Thomas Jefferson and in the text of the American Constitution. Following the pragmatism and positivism of our century, recent American jurists and philosophers are mostly contrary to the concept of natural law and believe that the decision of lawmakers and judges is sufficient to justify the validity of a law, of an action, or of a legal or moral judgment. If one asks on what foundation or principle a given law is based, they appeal to the

68. P. O. Kristeller, *Renaissance Thought and Its Sources* (New York: Columbia University Press, 1979), pp. 120 and 292n44.

69. Arnim 3, fr. 314. Arnim points to Marcianus, *Institut.*, book 1, as the source, but does not explicitly say that the direct source is the *Digest* (1.3.2) of Justinian.

70. P. O. Kristeller, "Stoic and Neo-Platonic Sources of Spinoza's Ethics," *History of European Ideas* 5 (1984):6 and 13n45; see also Kristeller, *Fonti antiche e rinascimentali dell'Etica dello Spinoza, In memoria di Giorgio Radetti* (Trieste: Circolo della cultura e delle arti, 1981), p. 13.

feeling not only of a single person but of a given society. They do not notice that the mere feeling of a society makes possible the most unjust actions of any tyrannical government, including that of the Nazis, and that in order to be able to criticize and condemn such a government and its legislation we need a more solid and more universal criterion than the feeling of an individual or a particular society. Justice has to be defined by a truly universal and rational criterion, and the concept of natural law formulated by the Stoics and transmitted and modified by the philosophers, theologians, and jurists of successive centuries through Kant seems the only way out of the dilemma to which positivism has brought us. If the concept of natural law in its traditional form carries with it difficulties and creates doubts, it should be corrected and modified, but not eliminated. It is one of the most precious legacies of ancient Stoicism and stands in profound agreement with the often crude, but profound and sincere ideals of our contemporary world.

CHAPTER THREE

Pyrrho and Arcesilaus

Aside from Epicureanism and Stoicism, a third philosophical current that had its origin in the Hellenistic age is Skepticism, which also has exercised a strong influence, both directly and indirectly, throughout the subsequent centuries until the present age. Like the Epicureans and the Stoics, the Skeptics also used and developed certain ideas of the pre-Socratics, of Socrates, of Plato, of Aristotle, and of their successors; but Skepticism, unlike Epicureanism and Stoicism, had no close link with an organized school, except for the limited period when Skeptic doctrine was adopted by the Academic school under Arcesilaus, Carneades, and their disciples. Ancient Skepticism, therefore, had no continuous tradition, but appears in various places and times, and the relationships among its different representatives are not always clear. The Skeptic doctrine has been transmitted to us in a complete and systematic form only by Sextus Empiricus, a relatively late author. The Skeptics of the Hellenistic age from Pyrrho and Arcesilaus to Carneades and Philo of Larissa have left us few authentic testimonies, and thus this part of our discourse will be less documented and more hypothetical than the others, leaving us more than ever exposed to the historical skepticism of those who do not believe that our presentation of the thinkers of the past is limited by the content of our sources and by their philological interpretation.

We find a few traces of skeptical thinking in the thought of Heraclitus, of the Sophists, and of Socrates himself, but the origins of Skepticism proper are linked to the name of Pyrrho of Elis, who lived approximately from 365 to 275 B.C. Of his life and teachings we know very little, but when the skeptic doctrine was abandoned by the Academy in the first century before Christ and was renewed outside the Academy by Aenesidemus and others, the new Skeptics called upon the almost legendary authority of Pyrrho to set themselves apart from the Academics, and the pure and non-Academic Skepticism was known as Pyrrhonism from the first century B.C. through the eighteenth century and beyond.

Of Pyrrho we know that he was a student of Bryso, who belonged to the Megarian school, and of Anaxarchus, a follower of Democritus, and that he accompanied him on the campaigns of Alexander the Great.[1] One of our sources affirms that Pyrrho had at that time contacts with the Gymnosophists

---

1. Diogenes Laertius, *Vitae et Placita philosophorum* 9.61; F. Decleva Caizzi, ed., *Pirrone: Testimonianze*, no. 1A.

of India and with the Magi of Persia.[2] Since the historians have often, and without a trace of evidence, spoken of the Eastern influences on Pythagoras, Plato, Plotinus, and other metaphysical and spiritual writers, it seems curious and even ironic that a specific testimony of just such an influence from the East, while not certain, should present itself among all others for the founder of Skepticism, a current far removed from those oriental mysteries that have held such fascination, unburdened by too many precise details, both for late Antiquity and for many circles of the present century. Anyway, an Eastern influence is not impossible in the case of Pyrrho since there are elements of Skepticism in Indian thought, even though there are none documented for such an early period.

Pyrrho taught, probably at Elis, and had many disciples. But it seems that he left no writings.[3] One of his students, Timon (circa 320–230 B.C.), composed several works in verse and prose and the fragments of Timon constitute our surest source for the thought of Pyrrho.

According to a source citing Timon, Pyrrho made the following statement: "He who wishes to be happy must look to three things: Of what kind things are, then what must be our attitude towards them and finally what the result of this attitude will be. To the first question the answer is that all things are indifferent, uncertain and unjudgable. For this reason neither our perceptions nor our opinions are either true or false. Hence, we cannot trust them, but must remain without opinion, without inclination and without involvement. Of everything it can be affirmed with equal validity that it is, that it is not, that it is and is not at the same time and that it neither is nor is not at

2. Decleva, no. 1A.
3. Diog. Laert. 9.102; Decleva, no. 44.

the same time. For those who reason in this way the first result is the absence of every affirmation, and the second is the tranquillity of the soul."[4] For tranquillity of the soul Timon uses the very word (*ataraxia*) used by Epicurus, and the absence of every affirmation (*aphasia*) means the liberation of the soul from all the opinions that could upset its tranquillity. So for Pyrrho, as for Epicurus and Zeno, the goal of his philosophical teaching is moral, and his epistemological doctrine, which insists on the uncertainty of all opinions, serves above all a moral end—namely, the liberation of our soul from those mistaken opinions that might imperil our happiness. We noted the same attitude in Epicurus, who also rejects erroneous opinions in questions of logic, of physics, and primarily of religion in order to protect the soul from the troubles that could result from them. But instead of stopping at this Skeptic position, Epicurus presents his own positive and dogmatic doctrine. The accent on the ethical value of Skeptic doctrine that we find in Pyrrho recurs frequently in the history of Skepticism (as it does in Montaigne for example), but this is not always brought out by the historians of Skepticism, who emphasize rather its negative theory of knowledge as an end in itself. Yet in the ancient tradition Pyrrho is primarily represented as an ethical model, as can be seen from the anecdotes reported of him.[5] He insists, along with the Stoics, on the indifference of the wise man before the external circumstances of life.[6] He does not bend before the passions and opinions

4. Eusebius, *Praeparatio Evangelica* 14.18; Decleva, no. 53; *Poetarum Philosophorum Fragmenta*, ed. H. Diels, Timon A 2, pp. 175–81.

5. Diog. Laert. 9.61–62; Decleva, nos. 6–10, 15B.

6. Diog. Laert. 9.66; Decleva, no. 15A; Cicero, *Academica Priora* 2.130; Decleva, no. 69A.

that dominate other men. Other men are full of empty and mistaken opinions from which only the wise man is free.[7]

"O Pyrrho," Timon addresses him, "how did you ever free yourself from the slavery of opinions, from the empty thought of the sophists and from the bond of every deceit or conviction?"[8] "Let me know, O Pyrrho, how you always behave with tranquillity, with ease and without anxiety or commotion, without heeding the snares of a sweetish wisdom, and how you alone rise up like a god above other men."[9]

Pyrrho introduces as the proper instrument to reach this freedom or moral indifference his epistemological principle, which he calls the absence of every affirmation or (using a term that would become more famous) *epokhe*, the suspension of every judgment.[10] We should not accept as true any particular opinion or doctrine since no proposition is any more true than its opposite.[11] One must determine nothing and give one's consent to nothing.[12] We must always distinguish between our experience or subjective perception and the objective fact in itself. I do not affirm that the honey is sweet, but I allow that it seems sweet. Wherever one turns, what dominates is only phenomenon or appearance.[13]

7. Decleva, nos. 69 A–M.

8. Diog. Laert. 9.64; Diels, no. B 48, pp. 196–97; *Supplementum Hellenisticum*, ed. H. Lloyd-Jones and P. Parsons, Timon no. 822, p. 385.

9. Diels, no. B 67, pp. 202–203; *Supplementum Hellenisticum*, no. 841, pp. 392–93.

10. Diog. Laert. 9.76. It is not certain that the term *epokhe* was used by Pyrrho himself.

11. Diog. Laert. 9.74–75; Gellius, *Noctes Atticae* 11.5.1–5 (Decleva, no. 56).

12. Diog. Laert. 9.76; Diels, no. B 80, p. 206.

13. Diog. Laert. 9.77, 103–105; Diels, no. B 74, p. 205.

So as to prevent this negation of every certainty from rendering the Skeptic incapable of acting and leading a normal life, he must follow nature and custom, though without any theoretical security. One must follow nature and custom, but not give one's consent to their theoretical validity.[14] As a purgative medicine eliminates the dirt and itself from the body, so Skeptic doctrine, which holds that all opinions are uncertain, eliminates, along with the other opinions, itself as well.[15] With this method one must attack all the natural philosophers and their assumptions.[16] It also seems that the name that the school bears, Skeptic, goes back to Pyrrho himself. The philosopher must consider and examine (*skeptesthai*) all opinions[17] and recognize that all affirmations have the same validity.[18]

It does not seem that Pyrrho developed his negative theory of knowledge and his critical ideas beyond the general principles we have discussed. Our sources mention the names of many Skeptic thinkers after Pyrrho, but we cannot affirm with certainty that a school or didactic tradition of his existed after Timon. Between Timon and Aenesidemus, who was the first to renew Pyrrhonian Skepticism (as opposed to Academic Skepticism), there is an interval of two centuries. This interval corresponds to the period in which the Academic school founded by Plato adopted a Skeptic tendency, following, but also transforming, the doctrine of Pyrrho. This Skeptic current, which began in the Academy with Arcesilaus, found it easy to absorb what had remained vital in Pyrrhonian Skepticism. Only later, when the Academy abandoned with Anti-

---

14. Eus., *Praep. Evang.* 14.18 and 20.
15. Diog. Laert. 9.76.
16. Diog. Laert. 9.70.
17. Diog. Laert. 9.69–70; Decleva, no. 39A.
18. Diog. Laert. 9.73–74.

ochus its Skeptic bent and returned to a dogmatic tendency, was there a need to revive Skepticism outside the Academy where it had lost its base and to return to the name and model of Pyrrho, founder of the Skeptic tradition and author of a doctrine about which little was known, but which was considered more pure than the Skepticism of the Academy. It is this so-called Pyrrhonian Skepticism that we find systematized in the writings of Sextus Empiricus and that had a notable influence—not in the Middle Ages when the works of Sextus were barely known, but from the sixteenth century onward. Many thinkers like Montaigne, Bayle, and Hume adopted a Skeptical position, and others like Gianfrancesco Pico, Descartes above all, and even Kant used Skeptic arguments to demolish certain philosophical doctrines.

Of the school of Pyrrho we know very little after the death of Timon (230 B.C.), but right around that time a different form of Skepticism, called Academic, was introduced into the Academy by Arcesilaus and held sway there in a modified form for almost two centuries.

The history of the Academy at the time of Plato and his immediate successors is relatively obscure and has been the object of much research and erudite controversy for almost a century. Plato is one of the few ancient philosophers (and perhaps the only one outside of Plotinus) all of whose writings have been preserved. And we know that they were almost continuously read, not only by professional philosophers but, because of their high literary quality, also by all those interested in classical Greek literature. These writings offer many difficulties that have puzzled interpreters and commentators from ancient times until today. Since the works of Plato are in dialogue form and are not bound together by any systematic order, the question always arises whether a doctrine expressed in a particular passage is put forward only in the course of the discussion or represents a position held and defended by Plato himself, or whether a doctrine clearly defended in one dialogue has been maintained also in other dialogues composed before or after it. Then there arises the question of the chronology of the dialogues, now largely resolved, and of the dubious authenticity of some dialogues attributed to Plato in Antiquity and in part even included in the ancient corpus of his writings. The situation has also been further complicated by the attempts of some distinguished scholars to postulate an oral and secret doctrine of Plato, not expressed in his dialogues but taught and traceable in the writings of Aristotle and in the fragments of the other disciples and followers of Plato. The effect of these theories has been to undermine the *Corpus Platonicum* as it is preserved as the solid foundation of our interpretation, so that even Plato has been added to the great number of ancient thinkers whose doctrines must be reconstructed on the basis of scattered fragments and testimonies with all the ingenious methods developed for that purpose by modern philology. We cannot completely ignore such theories, but I prefer to follow the example of Harold Cherniss and of my teacher, Ernst Hoffmann, and to base the interpretation of Plato on the preserved text of his dialogues, leaving to others the burden of proof for the existence of a lost Plato, one who is different and even contrary to the Plato of the dialogues.

Among the direct students of Plato, Aristotle, as is seen in his writings, underwent Plato's influence for many years, but then set out to develop many different and new doctrines while still a companion of Plato and a member of his Academy. The same goes for the other direct disciples—and especially for Speusippus and Xenocrates, who followed Plato as the leaders of the Academy and whose doctrines have been reconstructed on the basis of the usual testimonies and some fragments. Their doctrines were different on many points from that of Plato and even different from one another. It has been suggested by Cherniss and others, and it seems plausible to me, that the doctrines criticized by Aristotle and considered by modern scholars as oral and secret doctrines of Plato are in fact the explicit doctrines of the first Academics and different from those of Plato himself. As for Aristotle, he left the Academy after the death of Plato and founded his own Peripatetic school while the Academy was headed by his fellow disciples and rivals, Speusippus and Xenocrates.

The doctrine and teaching of Aristotle pose other serious problems for us, which we can only mention here. In the case of Aristotle we can affirm with certainty what for Plato has only been a chain of conjectures. He composed a great number of literary writings influenced by Plato and in part composed and published in his youth. These writings were widely circulated and read for several centuries after his death, but were lost in late Antiquity, and they have been reconstructed with the help of fragments and quotations, as has been done for the Pre-Socratics and for many Hellenistic thinkers. This reconstruction has served, especially in the work of Werner Jaeger and his students, to detail the chronological development of Aristotle's thought and the way in which he followed, modified, and criticized Plato in the various phases of his own thought.

We also have the *Corpus Aristotelicum* of the preserved writings, which constitutes a rich and complete encyclopedia of the philosophical and scientific disciplines and has been the basis of teaching and the subject of many commentaries by the later Aristotelians, by the ancient Neo-Platonists, by the Byzantine, Arabic, and Latin thinkers of the Middle Ages, and by many Aristotelian philosophers from the fifteenth to the seventeenth centuries and beyond. But a curious and often forgotten fact remains. The systematic writings of Aristotle were preserved and used by his disciples and successors within the Peripatetic school. Yet it seems that for many centuries they were not much read or available outside this school, and were published and made available to all only around the middle of the first century B.C. So we must consider as dubious and anachronistic the attempts of some scholars to derive the thought of Cicero, Philo of Alexandria, and other authors of the same period from influences of the *Corpus Aristotelicum* as we know it. These efforts are a consequence of what I like to call the pan-Aristotelianism of our century, based on a quite complete knowledge of the *Corpus Aristotelicum*, but also on an almost equally complete ignorance of ancient non-Aristotelian philosophy, particularly of Hellenistic (and neo-Platonic) philosophy. On the other hand, the Peripatetic school of Antiquity continued to preserve and enrich the doctrine of Aristotle for many centuries. We have not only fragments but complete and important texts of Theophrastus, Aristotle's successor as head of the Peripatetic school, and many interesting testimonies of Strato of Lampsacus and of the other members of the ancient Peripatetic school. Peripatetic doctrines, it seems, also had a significant influence on the other schools, and especially on the Academy and on the Stoa.

After this rather summary digression, we must return to the theme we have chosen for this lecture—namely, Academic Skepticism and its founder, Arcesilaus. He was born in Pitane in Aeolia toward 315 B.C., studied at Athens with Theophrastus and at the Academy with Polemon and Crantor. He was interested and knowledgeable in both mathematics and rhetoric and was influenced by Diodorus of Megara, the member of a minor Socratic school notable for its teaching in logic, as well as by Pyrrho, the founder of the Skeptic school. Arcesilaus became the head of the Academy after 270 and remained there until his death circa 240. He had considerable success with his teaching and he completely changed the direction of Plato's school, which up to that time had followed a dogmatic tradition and under him began to adopt a Skeptic position that would continue, with some modifications, for two centuries. So the ancient sources speak of a Second or Middle Academy beginning precisely with Arcesilaus.

Like Pyrrho, it seems Arcesilaus left no writings, though they say that his lectures were brought together and published by his pupil Pythodorus. But the testimonies that we do have on Arcesilaus probably derive from the oral tradition of the school itself.

According to Diogenes Laertius, Arcesilaus was the first to change Plato's doctrine as it had been passed down in the Academy, and he replaced it with a debate conducted through questions and answers. He taught the suspension of judgment (a doctrine taken from Pyrrho) by providing arguments for two contrary positions and claiming that these arguments were equally strong.[19] A contemporary writer of comedies said he was "Plato in front, Pyrrho in the back and Diodorus in the middle,"[20] thus asserting that Arcesilaus was only in appearance Platonic, but a Pyrrhonian in reality. While Diogenes Laertius does not offer us much more than a few anecdotes, we have some more solid materials in Eusebius, Sextus Empiricus, and a few other sources.

Arcesilaus affirms that we must suspend our assertions about everything. Every perception and every assertion (*logos*) is uncertain. The arguments in favor of contrary assertions are of equal force, and all things are incomprehensible (*akatalepta*).[21]

19. Diog. Laert. 4.28.
20. Diog. Laert. 4.33.
21. Eus., *Praep. Evang.* 14.5.

Incomprehensibility (*akatalepsia*), a term coined by Arcesilaus,[22] became a central concept in his doctrine, and it indicates that not only did he maintain a Skeptic and agnostic
position in general, as had been that of Pyrrho, but became
particularly critical of Zeno's dogmatic theory of knowledge
based on comprehending perception and on comprehension
as the sure criterion of valid knowledge and truth. For his
denial of what is true or false, and even probable, Arcesilaus
was called a Skeptic and, in all but name, a Pyrrhonian.[23]
Some authors go so far as to say that Arcesilaus only used
suspension of assertion as a polemical weapon and that he
kept to a secret and dogmatic Platonic doctrine,[24] but such
an opinion, contradicted by other sources, seems highly improbable to me, and I think it is due to later efforts to reconcile
the Middle and the Old Academy. Even Sextus Empiricus,
who insists on the difference between Pyrrhonian and Academic Skepticism, says that Arcesilaus essentially follows
Pyrrho since he suspends judgment on all things. But Sextus
does indicate an important feature that separates Arcesilaus
and Pyrrho. For Arcesilaus suspension is an end in itself,
and he calls particular suspensions good and particular as-
sents bad.[25] Arcesilaus's position is aimed pointedly at that
of Zeno (whose theory of knowledge assigns to assent as
well as to comprehension an important function); for Arcesilaus, epistemological Skepticism—that is, suspension—is an
end in itself, whereas our Skepticism (Pyrrhonian) persists
in saying that suspension carries with it the tranquillity of

22. Eus., *Praep. Evang.* 14.7.
23. Eus., *Praep. Evang.* 14.6.
24. Ibid.; Sextus Empiricus, *Pyrrhonianae Dissertationes* 1.234.
25. Sext. Emp., *Pyrrh. Diss.* 1.232–33.

the soul (*ataraxia*), which constitutes the true moral end of philosophy.[26]

We know of a few particular arguments directed by Arcesilaus against Zeno's doctrine. Zeno had stated that comprehension held an intermediate position between knowledge and opinion, a position that is incoherent even from the Stoic point of view, which makes comprehending perception identical to knowledge and opposed to opinion. Arcesilaus holds correctly that there is no intermediate act between knowledge and opinion.[27] Criticizing the concept of comprehending perception in itself, Arcesilaus insists that assent is not given to a perception or phantasy, but only to a proposition (*logos*).[28] What is more, and here the attack on Zeno's definition of comprehending phantasy is direct, there is no true phantasy that could not also be false. As a consequence all things are incomprehensible and the wise man must suspend all assent.[29]

Concerning practical life and happiness, the wise man who suspends all judgment orders his actions and his positive and negative choices according to a criterion Arcesilaus calls reasonable (*eulogon*). Happiness is based on prudence, prudence consists in correct acts (*katorthomata*), and an act is correct when it has a reasonable justification. The man who keeps to what is reasonable thus reaches a correct activity and arrives at happiness.[30] Arcesilaus takes the concept of the reasonable (*eulogon*) from Zeno himself and uses for correct action (*kator-*

26. Ibid.

27. Sextus Empiricus, *Adversus mathematicos* 7.153. See Zeno (Arnim 1, fr. 69).

28. Sext. Emp., *Adv. math.* 7.154.

29. Sext. Emp., *Adv. math.* 7.154–55.

30. Sext. Emp., *Adv. math.* 7.158.

thoma) the very definition that Zeno had given to the "proper" (*kathekon*), or that which has a reasonable justification.[31] This criterion of the reasonable has the same function for Arcesilaus that nature and custom had for the Pyrrhonian Skeptics, serving in practical life as an approximate guide, instead of the sure guide of reason that had been proposed by the dogmatic philosophers.

This brings up the question of whether Arcesilaus, when he introduces the reasonable (*eulogon*) as a practical guide, was anticipating the probabilism of his successor Carneades on this point. I believe we must give a negative reply to this question. The term used by Carneades for the probable is the plausible (*pithanon*) and not the reasonable (*eulogon*), and we have several testimonies that indicate that Arcesilaus also rejected the very concept of the plausible (*pithanon*) in an epistemological sense or as a criterion of truth. Eusebius and Sextus bear witness that Arcesilaus did not prefer one thing over another for being more or less probable,[32] and so the reasonable (*eulogon*) that he recognizes should be construed as what is practically more reasonable (and not as what is theoretically more plausible).

We find still more arguments proposed by Arcesilaus against Zeno. Zeno had affirmed that the wise man must not give his assent to any mere opinion.[33] Since there is no sure distinction between true knowledge (which may also be false) and mere opinions (which may be true or false), the wise man who wants to avoid false opinions must abstain from all opinions.[34] Arcesilaus also makes a direct attack on Zeno's criterion of

31. Zeno (Arnim 1, fr. 238).
32. Eus., *Praep. Evang.* 14.6; Sext. Emp., *Pyrrh. Diss.* 1.232.
33. Zeno (Arnim 1, fr. 54).
34. Cicero, *Acad. Pr.* 66–67; Sext. Emp., *Adv. math.* 7.155–57.

truth.[35] There is no perception based on truth that cannot also be based on what is false.[36] There is nothing that can be known with certainty, not even what Socrates had left intact when speaking of himself, namely that he knew that he knew nothing. Nothing can be perceived or known, hence no one must affirm anything or approve of it with assent. One must always abstain from assent and always restrain one's temerity in order to avoid every error.[37] So Arcesilaus would criticize the doctrines of all philosophers. Since the contrary opinions on the same question are sustained by arguments of equal weight, the easiest thing is to withhold one's assent from both opinions.

It seems that Arcesilaus justified his method with the example of Socrates and Plato themselves. He interpreted the discourses of Socrates and the dialogues of Plato in the sense that in things that can be perceived by the senses or by the soul there is nothing certain. Not revealing what he thought himself, Socrates (and Plato too) set out to argue against that which all the others were affirming. There is talk of a New Academy, but it should be called old if we think of Plato as the founder of the Old Academy, since in his dialogues nothing is affirmed, many things are discussed according to two contrary positions, everything is doubted, and nothing certain is maintained.[38] In this way Arcesilaus avoided appearing as the inventor of new doctrines and attributed even his doctrines of suspension and of non-comprehension to Socrates and Plato, and even to Heraclitus and Parmenides.[39] It hap-

35. Zeno (Arnim 1, fr. 59).

36. Cic., *Acad. Pr.* 77; Sext. Emp., *Adv. math.* 7.154.

37. Cicero, *Academica Posteriora* 2.45.

38. Cic., *Acad. Post.* 2.46; Cicero, *De oratore* 3.67.

39. Plutarch, *Adversus Colotem* 26.

pens that Arcesilaus proposed a Skeptic interpretation of Plato himself in order to justify his own Skeptic position. This Skeptic interpretation of Plato (which I find wrong) has found many followers among those modern scholars who were opposed to the theory of ideas and to Platonic metaphysics, and we must note that this modern interpretation of Plato had its origins in ancient tradition, and especially in the teaching of Arcesilaus and of his Academy.

We can ascribe some other doctrines to Arcesilaus on the basis of the criticisms directed against him by Chrysippus in defense of the position of Zeno. We know from an explicit source that Chrysippus wrote a book against Arcesilaus,[40] and the opinion of some authoritative scholars of Epicurus that Chrysippus directed his polemical arguments only against Epicurus and made no mention of Arcesilaus is evidently mistaken. In fact, all the arguments of Chrysippus that defend Zeno against his Skeptic critics have Arcesilaus in mind, even when his name is not explicitly mentioned.

Whereas Zeno had held that an act of assent is required between perception and consecutive action, it seems that Arcesilaus thought that one could go directly from perception to action without any need for an intermediary assent, a position later rejected by Chrysippus.[41] Arcesilaus also criticized the Stoic concept of the existing object that produces comprehending perception.[42] Attacking Stoic physics as well, Arcesilaus criticized the concept of complete mixture and denied the doctrine that said that no piece of grain, however similar to

40. Diog. Laert. 7.198; Arnim 2, fr. 8, line 20.

41. Arnim 3, fr. 177 (Plutarch, *De Stoicorum repugnantiis* 47). See also Plut., *Adv. Col.* 26.

42. Arnim 2, fr. 69 (Sext. Emp., *Adv. math.* 7.426).

another one, is completely identical to it.[43] Arcesilaus also made use of many sophisms and especially the Sorites against the position of Zeno, trying to prove that there was a gradual passage from the last comprehending perception to the first non-comprehending perception.[44] He also tried to refute the argument that the Skeptic position destroyed itself because the general uncertainty applied as well to the very affirmation of uncertainty itself.[45] It seems that Arcesilaus set out to prove that the concepts of possibility, of free will and of free assent, and of good and evil were incompatible with the Stoic concept of fate.[46] In particular he used a famous argument against Stoic determinism called the inactive reasoning (*argos logos*), according to which man must abstain from every free good or bad action since the consequence of his action is determined by fate in any case.[47] He insisted also that the possibility of any moral progress was excluded by the total contrast between the wise man and the fool that characterizes Zeno's teaching.[48] Arcesilaus also criticized the very concept of the wise man, saying that the wise man, as Zeno defines him, is nowhere to be found,[49] and that the wise man, even if he does exist, can be recognized as such neither by others nor by himself.[50]

A more detailed investigation of the passages in which Plutarch and Sextus criticize the Stoics might reveal still other

43. Arnim 2, fr. 113 (Cic., *Acad. Pr.* 93).

44. Arnim 2, fr. 276 (Sext. Emp., *Adv. math.* 7.416) and 277 (Cic., *Acad. Pr.* 93).

45. Arnim 2, fr. 118 and 121.

46. Arnim 2, fr. 959–964 and 974ff.

47. Arnim 2, fr. 956–958.

48. Arnim 3, fr. 539.

49. Arnim 3, fr. 545, 657, and 662.

50. Arnim 3, fr. 539 and 568.

anti-Stoic arguments that go back to Arcesilaus. But from what we have collected we can see already that Arcesilaus must have furnished a whole arsenal of interesting arguments that could be used by critics of the Stoic doctrine for a long time, even outside the school of the Academy.

Among the students of Arcesilaus, the best known is Lacydes of Cyrene, who succeeded him as the head of the Academy. We learn that he carried on the doctrines of Arcesilaus, especially those on suspension and incomprehension.[51] Since some published writings by him are mentioned, it may be that some of the testimonies that we do have on Arcesilaus' doctrine derive from the writings of Lacydes. On the other hand, Lacydes is occasionally called the founder of a new Academy,[52] but we know of no specific doctrine of his that would justify the attempt to assign him such an important role in the history of the Academy and of its doctrine. The radically Skeptic phase of the school remains connected with the name of Arcesilaus, and a new phase, from what we know, did not begin until Carneades, who became the head of the Academy about eighty years after the death of Arcesilaus.

The historical importance of Arcesilaus consists in the fact that with him the Academy of Plato took a Skeptic direction that was to last, with some modifications, for almost two centuries and that he offered a Skeptic interpretation of Plato himself. Such an interpretation, though not destined to last in the subsequent history of Platonism, reappears many times in the history—even the recent history—of the commentaries on Plato. One should keep in mind that the authority of the Academic school under Arcesilaus and his successors, well known through the writings of Cicero, contributed signifi-

---

51. Eus., *Praep. Evang.* 14.7; Diog. Laert. 4.59–61.
52. Diog. Laert. 4.59.

cantly to the influence of Skepticism in the following centuries, despite the criticism directed against the Academics by the purer Skeptics of the Pyrrhonian school.

The criticism of Arcesilaus was directed in the first place against Zeno and his immediate followers. It is understandable that Arcesilaus, finding himself up against a new and effective rival school, instead of directly defending the doctrine of his predecessors and of Plato himself, preferred to refute the new doctrine with Skeptic arguments. And he did provoke the Stoics to defend themselves against his arguments. Indeed, Chrysippus, the third and greatest head of the Stoa in Antiquity, not only defended the doctrine of Zeno against Arcesilaus and other critics, but he also modified, developed, and expanded it in many essential points. In the next lecture we propose to describe the principal features of the Stoic doctrine of Chrysippus, focusing on the way that he enlarged and even changed Zeno's doctrine, as well as on the way in which this definitive transformation of ancient Stoicism was motivated by the intention to define and strengthen the doctrine of Zeno against Arcesilaus and its other critics.

CHAPTER FOUR

Chrysippus

Chrysippus of Soloi, the third head of the Stoic school, was more important than his predecessors, including Zeno himself. He presented the doctrines of Zeno in a more explicit and refined way, filled its gaps, bolstered his position with subtle defenses against the objections of Arcesilaus and other contemporaries, and enriched it with many ideas, some of them new, some derived from the opponents themselves. His great merits were recognized and are reflected even in a popular verse: "If there had been no Chrysippus, there would be no

Stoa."[1] His literary style was criticized as pedantic and lacking in elegance. We have by him few verbatim preserved fragments as we do for Epicurus and Cleanthes. But the number and the mass of the testimonies that describe his doctrine are greater than for any other thinker, Hellenistic or otherwise, whose writings have not been preserved. This fact is due in part to Arnim, who attributed to Chrysippus all testimonies on ancient Stoicism not explicitly attributed to Zeno or to his immediate disciples. But this approach is probably justified since we know that Chrysippus left many writings and since so many of the Stoic teachings not attributed to Zeno are linked by one or another of our sources to the name of Chrysippus. The wealth of the direct and indirect testimonies forces us to choose for our presentation only the principal doctrines and to omit many subtle and interesting points.

Chrysippus was born in Soloi in Cilicia circa 280 B.C., became head of the Stoic school in Athens toward 232, and died around 205.

In his logic Chrysippus considers phantasy as a criterion of truth, but he distinguishes clearly between phantasy as a subject, its object (*phantaston*), the representation without an object (*phantastikon*), and its imaginary object (*phantasma*).[2] Zeno had defined comprehending perception as that which refers to an existing object. His critics, and especially Arcesilaus, had rebutted that there is no criterion to distinguish between perceptions derived from an existing object and those without such a basis. Chrysippus responds with a circular and rather unconvincing argument which does, however, reveal the point

1. Arnim 2, fr. 6 (Diogenes Laertius, *Vitae et Placita philosophorum* 7.183). (All references to Arnim in this chapter are to H. von Arnim, *Stoicorum Veterum Fragmenta*, 4 vols.).

2. Arnim 2, fr. 54.

of the discussion: existent is that which produces a comprehending perception.[3] Chrysippus clarifies certain ambiguities in Zeno's concept of the comprehending phantasy and of comprehension. He distinguishes perception (*aisthesis*) from phantasy and affirms that perception includes both the phantasy and the assent to it,[4] and that comprehension includes the assent to the comprehending phantasy.[5] He describes the governing part of our soul (*hegemonikon*) as a tabula rasa upon which all our notions (*ennoiai*) are inscribed. These notions derive either from perception and memory or from teaching.[6] Those that derive from perception and memory are called anticipations (*prolepseis*),[7] a term that Chrysippus takes from Epicurus and which serves to explain how universal concepts are formed on the basis of repeated perceptions that are common to all human beings. Notions (*ennoiai*) are the phantasies of rational animals, while the other animals, lacking a rational soul, have no notions, only phantasies.[8] In order to defend the doctrine of comprehension against Arcesilaus, Chrysippus holds that there are no two existing objects that are completely identical,[9] a doctrine denied by Arcesilaus but one that was taken up again many centuries later by Leibniz. Chrysippus also urged the point against Arcesilaus that Skeptic doctrine refuted even itself and was, therefore, contradictory.[10]

Chrysippus adds to Stoic logic several new concepts that

3. Arnim 2, fr. 69.
4. Arnim 2, fr. 72–74.
5. Arnim 2, fr. 91.
6. Arnim 2, fr. 83.
7. Ibid.
8. Ibid.
9. Arnim 2, fr. 113.
10. Arnim 2, fr. 118, 121.

would have notable influence on many later developments. He insists on the distinction between the signifier and the signified,[11] as well as between the concept as thought (*logos endiathetos*) and the pronounced word (*logos prophorikos*).[12] The word (*phone*) is only a bit of air set in movement, and therefore it is corporeal.[13] Words are natural and not conventional or arbitrary.[14] Chrysippus distinguishes five parts of speech: noun, preposition, verb, conjunction, and article.[15] Here we have an analysis of Greek speech that was to serve as the starting point for the Greek grammarians of the Alexandrian age. It would also, with some modification, provide the basis for the theory of the parts of speech in Latin grammar and in the grammar of the modern languages until recent times.

Of central importance was Chrysippus' distinction between the signifier and the signified. The signifier for him is the word, the signified is the thing indicated by the word. And there is a third factor—the object that exists outside, to which the word refers, and that Chrysippus calls the real (*tunkhanon*). Of these three factors two are corporeal—that is, the word and the real—but the signified or the spoken (*lekton*) is incorporeal.[16] This distinction is new and historically important and derives from Stoic nominalism. For Plato and even for Aristotle there is no reason to distinguish between the meaning of a word or a concept and the real object to which it refers. The concept of 'horse' means the generic horse that really exists—for Plato as an idea separate from particular objects, and for

11. Arnim 2, fr. 122.
12. Arnim 2, fr. 135.
13. Arnim 2, fr. 139–142.
14. Arnim 2, fr. 146.
15. Arnim 2, fr. 147–148.
16. Arnim 2, fr. 166, 168.

Aristotle as a species or genus that is really present or inherent in the individual horse. Instead, for Stoic nominalism the generic horse is nothing but a generic concept signified by the word 'horse,' and the question if or where in the external world a real object is found to which the word and its concept refer remains open. This logical and epistemological position, completely different from that of Aristotle, recurs with some modification in other philosophical periods, and we do not know with certainty if there was a direct influence by Stoic logic or if a certain way of thinking spontaneously produced an analogous solution to the respective problems. Also, the terministic logic of the Middle Ages, which begins in the thirteenth century at the time of Petrus Hispanus, distinguishes the word both from its concept and from the external things to which it may refer, attributing to every word or term a *significatio* corresponding to a pure concept without any pretense of real existence, and a *suppositio* indicating the real objects to which the word and the concept may be applied. The important thing here is the definition of *suppositio,* and the often repeated fact that this *suppositio* changes with the proposition of which the concept is a part is a subsequent theorem that does not touch the definition as such. Similarly, the distinction is made in certain sectors of modern logic between meaning and reference, that is, between the logical meaning of a word or concept and its reference to an existing reality. Many contemporary thinkers and historians are so partial to Aristotle and so ignorant of the other philosophical currents of classical Antiquity (a tendency which I term pan-Aristotelianism) that they are ready to attribute to Aristotle all the doctrines they hold to be valid—whence the attempt to link Aristotle with certain aspects of modern logic that he had nothing to do with, while the ancient source or analogy, Stoic logic, is denied or forgotten.

Chrysippus distinguishes eight forms of the proposition, of

which the principal form, which may be true or false, is called axiom.[17] He insists that besides the categorical syllogism discussed by Aristotle there are also hypothetical and disjunctive syllogisms.[18] It seems he developed a new and detailed theory of these syllogisms, but we do not know its particulars. Here too Chrysippus anticipated modern logic, which has dedicated much attention to hypothetical syllogisms.

Chrysippus also studied various forms of sophisms and especially the one named the Sorites, evidently in response to certain of Arcesilaus' arguments. When the wise man is pushed by his adversary to concede that there is a gradual passage from the last comprehending perception to the first non-comprehending one, Chrysippus exhorts him just to stop and keep his peace of mind,[19] a counsel that really does not solve the problem and, witty as it is, substantially amounts to a capitulation.

Also, Stoic physics was completed and developed by Chrysippus. With Zeno, he posits God and matter as the two fundamental principles of the world, both of them material, and he insists that God has as matter a subtle substance called spirit (*pneuma*) composed of fire and air.[20] In spite of his general materialism, Chrysippus posits four incorporeal things— namely, the void (recognized as incorporeal by Epicurus also), place or space (*topos*), time, and meaning (*lekton*).[21] The notion (*ennoema*) stands in between and is neither corporeal nor incorporeal.[22] The distinction between corporeal and incorporeal leads to the conclusion that being is not the most general

17. Arnim 2, fr. 193.
18. Arnim 2, fr. 217.
19. Arnim 2. fr. 276.
20. Arnim 2, fr. 310.
21. Arnim 2, fr. 331.
22. Arnim 2. fr. 329.

category in the universe, but that 'whatness' or quiddity (*ti*) is more general than being. The category of being is valid only for corporeal things, whereas that of whatness is also good for incorporeal things.[23] Also Plotinus and his successors will not accept being as the most universal concept, putting above it the one and the good.

Instead of the four causes of Aristotle, Chrysippus posits the four following causes: occasional causes, sufficient causes, concurrent causes, and necessary causes.[24] The distinction between necessary causes and sufficient causes is particularly important. Even in the current discussions of an ideological or political nature it is often ignored, and when it is shown that a certain economic, social, or psychological factor is necessary for certain developments and for certain ideas, the belief is that it has been shown also to be the sufficient cause. This is not true because it usually takes many causes and many factors to explain a historical or intellectual phenomenon.

Among the corporeal things that have some form of unity, Chrysippus distinguishes between those composed of separate parts (like an army), of contiguous parts (like a house), and of united parts (like an animal).[25] The fundamental categories are not ten, as in Aristotle, but four: substrates, qualities, things set in a certain way, and things set in a certain way toward something.[26] This final category corresponds, it seems, to relation, while the third category stands for the seven Aristotelian categories as distinct from substance, quality, and relation. The qualities are all corporeal,[27] and there are four

23. Ibid.
24. Arnim 2, fr. 346.
25. Arnim 2, fr. 366.
26. Arnim 2, fr. 369.
27. Arnim 2, fr. 380.

principal qualities—two active (hot and cold) and two passive (dry and humid).[28] Chrysippus posits the usual four elements that compose all bodies, but in an another sense fire is the only element from which the others are composed and to which they return.[29] All bodies are bound to one another by the spirit capable of uniting itself and all other things.[30] This spirit penetrates all things and mixes with everything.[31] The spirit has a tension of its own and thanks to this all bodies have a double tension, one directed inward and the other directed outward. The equilibrium between these two opposite tensions produces an apparent state of equilibrium and rest.[32]

Like Aristotle and others, Chrysippus distinguishes between men, animals, and plants, assigning to them respectively reason (*logos*), soul (characterized by perception and movement, *horme*), and nature (*phusis*). He then adds as a lower level inanimate bodies like minerals, to which he attributes a principle of cohesion (*hexis*).[33]

In order to maintain the corporeal character of the soul and of the qualities, Chrysippus postulates a total mixture between the gross and the subtle particles that form all bodies, so that there is no part of the body that does not contain both types of particles.[34] This total mixture is different from other forms of mixture, such as juxtaposition or the mixture of liquid parts.[35]

28. Arnim 2, fr. 406.
29. Arnim 2, fr. 413.
30. Arnim 2, fr. 440.
31. Arnim 2, fr. 442.
32. Arnim 2, fr. 450–454.
33. Arnim 2, fr. 458–460.
34. Arnim 2, fr. 467.
35. Arnim 2, fr. 472.

Place or space are defined as that which is completely occupied by being.[36] Time is defined, with a modification of Zeno's formula, as the extension that corresponds to the movement of the world.[37] Chrysippus distinguishes between the universe that also includes the external void and the world which constitutes its center.[38] So the world is single and finite and includes the celestial and elementary spheres.[39] This world is generated and destroyed by fire in periodic cycles, but this fire is considered as splendor and not as destructive flame.[40]

The world is conceived as a rational animal whose upper part is the sky.[41] The human soul is corporeal, is a part of the world soul, and returns to it after death. Only the souls of the wise survive the death of their bodies, but even they persist only until the next conflagration.[42] The immortality of the soul is denied by the Stoics. The governing part of the soul has its seat in the heart and to it belongs perception.[43]

The world's reason is the fate that governs everything without obstacle.[44] Fate serves to justify soothsaying and mantic predictions since the effects are determined by their causes.[45] A critic of Zeno, probably Arcesilaus, had used against fate the argument of inactivity (*argos logos*), according to which we should do nothing since everything is predetermined and will necessarily occur and it makes no difference whether we de-

36. Arnim 2, fr. 503.

37. Arnim 2. fr. 509.

38. Arnim 2, fr. 522.

39. Arnim 2, fr. 530–531, 534ff.

40. Arnim 2, fr. 596–626.

41. Arnim 2, fr. 633ff., 642ff.

42. Arnim 2, fr. 790, 811, 821.

43. Arnim 2, fr. 854, 885.

44. Arnim 2, fr. 913, 935.

45. Arnim 2, fr. 939ff.

cide to do something or not to. Chrysippus tries to avoid this argument by introducing the concept of fatal components.[46] This means that fate springs from more than one determining factor, and our decision to do something is to be considered as one of the component factors. The argument seems inconclusive to me, but again it shows Chrysippus trying to confront the problems inherent in Zeno's doctrine. In a similar way he is attempting to defend the presence of the possible in a system dominated by fate. Nothing prevents events contrary to what fate ordains from actually happening. They do not happen, but the possibility remains that they may.[47] Chrysippus even offers a definition of chance without assigning it an active role in the world, as had the Epicureans. According to Chrysippus, chance (*tukhe*) is a cause unknown to human reason. This formula allows us to speak of ordinary events due to fate, but it indicates that some progress of our knowledge may enable us to understand as necessary what at first glance seems fortuitous.[48]

Chrysippus also tries to reconcile free will with the deterministic doctrine of fate. He distinguishes between antecedent causes and necessary causes. Everything happens according to antecedent causes and, therefore, according to fate, but the necessary and more immediate causes also include our free decisions. Free will (*eph'hemin*) would thus be compatible with fate, from which it follows that the movements of the animals happen on the basis of fate, but through the animals and through the choice of the animals. Decision and action on our part are included in fate itself, and the same is true for good and evil, praise and blame, reward and punishment for our

46. Arnim 2, fr. 956ff.
47. Arnim 2, fr. 959ff.
48. Arnim 2, fr. 965ff.

actions.[49] I do not find these ingenious arguments entirely convincing, but they do represent a first attempt to defend determinism and to confront the difficult problems inherent in that doctrine. Such arguments have been repeated and rephrased in modified form for many centuries down to our time and have been transferred from the philosophical context where they originated to the theological and scientific context. We find them again in Pomponazzi, in the Reformation debates on predestination and in the modern discussions on determinism in the physical, biological, and psychological sciences, and even in today's debates, more lively than scientific, on the economic, social, and political problems of our age.

The final part of physics for Chrysippus and the other Stoic thinkers is theology. He presents various arguments for the existence of the gods and identifies the supreme God with the world soul.[50] Only the supreme God is eternal while the other gods are corruptible, but he too is corporeal.[51] However, the Stoic gods do not have human form like those of the Epicureans.[52] After the model of the sophists and of Plato, Chrysippus favors an allegorical interpretation of popular religion, identifying the other gods with various natural forces[53] and the supreme God with nature[54] (as did Bruno and Spinoza). This nature is defined as an artificial fire that is moved by itself and proceeds to the generation of all things.[55] The whole

49. Arnim 2, fr. 974ff.
50. Arnim 2, fr. 1011ff., 1028ff.
51. Arnim 2, fr. 1028ff., 1049ff.
52. Arnim 2, fr. 1057ff.
53. Arnim 2, fr. 1061ff.
54. Arnim 2, fr. 936, 945, 1024, 1076, and passim.
55. Arnim 2, fr. 423, 1027, 1133.

world is the product of divine and natural providence, and all the animals and plants were created for the benefit of man.[56] This Stoic concept of providence was bound to please the Christian writers, but it is not clear how it could be harmonized and combined with their conceptions of fate and nature.

The question arises how the various forms of evil encountered in the world can be reconciled with a divine providence that was supposed to direct everything toward the good. Here we are facing the problem of theodicy or divine justice, and again it seems that Chrysippus was the first to confront this problem too. He proposed intelligent, if not conclusive, arguments that were to be repeated and developed by the philosophers and theologians of the following ages until the eighteenth century.[57] We learn that in a complete world there must be contrasts,[58] and that some disadvantages are the inevitable consequences of greater advantages necessary for a good world.[59] He also uses the argument, familiar from the Bible, that the misfortunes and even the catastrophic events befalling the world are the punishment of mankind for its transgressions.[60] These events, however bad when considered in themselves, are part of the general economy of the world.[61] One should pay no heed to small evils,[62] while even greater evil is not without its usefulness for the whole world; without the contrast of evil even the good could not exist, just as bad lines

56. Arnim 2, fr. 1141ff., 1152ff.
57. Arnim 2, fr. 1168ff.
58. Arnim 2, fr. 1169.
59. Arnim 2, fr. 1170.
60. Arnim 2, fr. 1174.
61. Arnim 2. fr. 1176.
62. Arnim 2, fr. 1178.

contribute to the quality of a good play.[63] In short, looking at the world as a whole, it is neither possible nor desirable for evil to be completely eliminated.[64]

As with all the Stoics and with Epicurus, for Chrysippus ethics is the most important part of philosophy, being closer to life,[65] while physics serves primarily as an introduction to ethics and as a foundation for it.[66] Life according to virtue is also life according to the experience of natural things since our natures are parts of the nature of the universe;[67] hence the moral end is the life according to nature, that is, according to our nature and according to the nature of the universe. On this point Chrysippus clarifies and changes the definitions given by Zeno and Cleanthes.[68] Virtue is an end in itself and is the opposite of pleasure. Criticizing Epicurus, Chrysippus even rejects as an end the combination of virtue with pleasure and says that a virtue pursued for the reward of pleasure is not true virtue, but a false imitation of it.[69]

In the same sense one must interpret the famous Stoic saying that only the beautiful is good (*monon to kalon agathon*).[70] The beautiful does not mean aesthetic beauty as in the majority of ancient authors including Plato. For Chrysippus it means the strictly moral good. For this reason the term *kalon* was translated by Cicero not by *pulchrum* but by *honestum*, a rendering that has engendered many misunderstandings by identi-

63. Arnim 2, fr. 1181.
64. Arnim 2, fr. 1182.
65. Arnim 3, fr. 69.
66. Arnim 3, fr. 68.
67. Arnim 3, fr. 4.
68. Arnim 3, fr. 12, 16.
69. Arnim 3, fr. 21.
70. Arnim 3, fr. 29ff. (see also fr. 75 and 83).

fying and confusing the moral good with honor and with honesty. The good (*agathon*), on the other hand, is understood by Chrysippus, according to common Greek usage, as what is good or useful. So he understood the Stoic maxim in the sense that only the moral good is good. Unlike other philosophers such as Plato and Aristotle, the doctrine of the Stoics excludes from the concept of the good all the other things commonly considered good and limits the concept of the good exclusively to the moral good. Despite the use of beautiful, a rather ambiguous word, the Stoic doctrine has made here a clearer and more rigid distinction between the moral good and the other kinds of good than had common usage or the preceding philosophers. It can be said that this clarification dominated the whole subsequent tradition of philosophy, including those thinkers who did not follow the Stoic doctrine on other particular points. Only Kant adopted the Stoic position in all its rigidity and then went beyond the Stoics, rejecting as an end even happiness, whereas the Stoics (who refused pleasure as an end) recognized with all other ancient philosophers happiness as an end, insisting only that happiness is obtained through virtue alone. The beautiful is identified by Chrysippus with virtue, which is desired for itself and which carries its own reward in itself and is sufficient by itself to obtain happiness, and is even identical with happiness (as vice is identical with misery).[71]

Chrysippus, following Epicurus, also affirms that happiness is not increased by time;[72] but elsewhere he says that a happiness that only lasts a while is not worth much.[73] Good and

71. Arnim 3, fr. 39ff., 49ff., 55, 57.
72. Arnim 3, fr. 54.
73. Arnim 3, fr. 210.

evil are corporeal and perceptible things,[74] and all goods are equal,[75] remembering that the goods considered minor in common usage are not recognized by the Stoics as goods. Chrysippus posits three kinds of goods and modifies the conventional scheme according to the Stoic criteria. The goods of the soul are the virtues and good actions, the external goods are the friends, and a third type of good is the wise man because he is useful to himself.[76] In the middle, between good and evil, are the things that are indifferent (*adiaphora*), and to this group belong all things considered good in common usage, like wealth and good health. These so-called goods can be either useful or harmful according to circumstances and can be used well or poorly, hence they are not goods but morally indifferent.[77] Among the indifferent things some are preferable and others not preferable. Wealth and good health, though not good but indifferent, are preferable to poverty and sickness.[78] Stoic doctrine, as rigid as it is in its insistence on pure virtue, lends itself in this way, when applied in practice, to a certain more or less hypocritical opportunism, since in all those situations (and they are numerous) where there is no choice between clearly good or evil actions, but between various morally indifferent alternatives, we can choose those actions that lead us to preferable things like wealth or health and so cater to our own selfish advantage, as we observed already in the case of Zeno.

In Stoic ethics an important place is held by the theory of appetite (*horme*). According to Chrysippus, the appetite that

74. Arnim 3, fr. 84–85.
75. Arnim 3, fr. 92.
76. Arnim 3, fr. 96–97.
77. Arnim 3, fr. 117.
78. Arnim 3, fr. 127ff.

leads to action always includes an act of assent.[79] The fundamental appetite common to all animals is directed toward
self-preservation, and not to pleasure, as Epicurus believed.
Pleasure is only a secondary accident that comes with self-
preservation and its consciousness. Human beings share this
appetite with the animals, but reason is added and with it the
end of living according to reason.[80]

Like Epicurus, Chrysippus considers wisdom as an art of
living, and he likes to compare virtue with medicine, music,
and the other arts. Virtue is like the art of the flute player, and
the life of the wise man is a system of rational actions just as
art is a system of valid knowledge. The wise man practices the
medicine of the soul and possesses an art of living which
determines all his actions in the best possible way.[81] Being an
art of living, virtue can be learned and taught.[82] But the actual
virtue taught by philosophy is preceded by an appetite for
virtue that we all possess and which is natural to us. We all
have from nature a preparation and a progress (*prokope*) toward
all the virtues, and we are predisposed by nature to the moral
good.[83]

Since we are predisposed by nature to virtue, we must ask
why we are capable of vice and bad actions. As an explanation
Chrysippus introduces what he calls distortion (*diastrophe*), an
irrational impulse that moves against our natural, good inclination.[84] This concept does not offer a true solution to the

79. Arnim 3, fr. 177.
80. Arnim 3, fr. 178ff.
81. Arnim 3, fr. 202, 204, 214, 293, 471, 516, 521, 560.
82. Arnim 3, fr. 223.
83. Arnim 3, fr. 214, 217.
84. Arnim 3, fr. 228ff.

problem, but it indicates its presence, and it can be compared to the original sin of St. Augustine and to the radical evil of Kant.

Chrysippus outlines four principal virtues—prudence, temperance, justice, and fortitude (the cardinal virtues of tradition)—and many subdivisions of them, and he defines them all as forms of knowledge and of disposition,[85] but he affirms with Zeno that all the virtues are inseparable since one virtue follows another, and he who has one of them has them all.[86] They are all corporeal and identical with the principal faculty of the soul.[87] The just and the other things that are good are so by nature and not by convention,[88] as was also the opinion of Aristotle and the other ancient philosophers excepting the sophists.

The concept of natural law (which is separate from this concept of the just by nature) was introduced by Zeno and developed by Chrysippus. The world is one big city and has only one constitution and only one law that commands what should be done and prohibits what should not.[89] Single peoples and states each have their law and customs, but they are all based on the universal law to which each adds something.[90] Natural law is universal and bound with the world's nature and soul. This is a specifically Stoic concept whose universal

85. Arnim 3, fr. 262ff.

86. Arnim 3, fr. 295ff.

87. Arnim 3, fr. 305.

88. Arnim 3, fr. 308.

89. Arnim 3, fr. 314. It should be noted (and Arnim does not explicitly do so) that these first sentences from Chrysippus' book on law are cited and preserved in their original Greek text in Justinian's *Corpus Iuris* (*Digest* 1.3.2).

90. Arnim 3, fr. 323, 324, 326.

validity has a cosmological basis and character and which has no analogy in the thought of Aristotle or of other ancient philosophers. It is a law that applies to all human beings beyond the positive laws of the various peoples, but vice versa the various positive laws derive their validity from the natural law of the world and from their agreement with it. Particular positive law, when not in agreement with universal law, is based only on the particular legislation of the respective people and is to be obeyed by the members of that society, but it does not automatically apply to all the other peoples.

This Stoic (and not Aristotelian) concept of natural law had a profound influence on the thought of the Roman jurists, including Cicero, and the opening words of Chrysippus' treatise on law (which are quite eloquent, unlike his usual prosaic style) were preserved literally in the original Greek by a Roman jurist. And they are quoted from this writer in the same text of Justinian's *Digest* preserved in the famous ancient codex called the Pisan or Florentine: "Law [*nomos*] is the king of all things divine and human; it is the governor and regent of things beautiful and ugly, it is the canon of things just and unjust that commands to the animals political by nature what should be done and prohibits what should not be done."[91] This concept, transmitted by Roman law to modern times, was accepted not only by the jurists and philosophers of the Middle Ages but also by Grotius, Spinoza, and other thinkers until the eighteenth century, and is still implicit in the laws on human rights of the French and American constitutions and in some recent documents of the United Nations. It was transformed by St. Augustine according to certain neo-Platonic conceptions into a divine law inherent in the mind of God, as the natural law had been inherent in the mind of the world soul,

91. Arnim 3, fr. 314 (see note 89 above).

the divine principle recognized by the Stoic philosophers. The tendency of modern American jurists and philosophers to reject natural law as an essentially theological concept (which it is not) and to base law exclusively on legislation and on the decisions of the judges guided by the feeling for what is just that prevails in their mind or in contemporary society is potentially dangerous because we have no guarantee that individual or public feelings may not be contrary to true justice. Indeed, in our century we have seen more than one example of the perversion of justice on the basis of laws or decisions corresponding to the feelings of those in government and their followers, but contrary to fundamental law. We need a juridical and also moral principle that is universal and that can serve as a canon for particular decisions, even if the particular legislation or decision is never completely determined by the general rule. The Stoic formula is especially precious because it is based on an empirical and materialistic system and does not assume those Kantian ideal and a priori principles that are valid for me but denied by the majority of our contemporaries.

Chrysippus defines the city or republic as a group of human beings governed by a law,[92] and adds that the world is a city or republic of which the gods and all men are part.[93] Therefore all human beings constitute a natural community, and the just man is by definition a citizen of the world, a cosmopolitan.[94] The concept and the term "cosmopolitan" were of Stoic coinage, and it seems strange that an illustrious historian of philosophy should tie the origins of this concept to Christian sources without even mentioning the Stoics. This reflects the usual

92. Arnim 3, fr. 327.
93. Arnim 3, fr. 333.
94. Arnim 3, fr. 336.

modern tendency to attribute to Biblical or Christian sources all philosophical concepts that are not of Aristotelian origin. Even in our political and pedagogical discourses one often hears it said that all our moral concepts have their origin in the tradition called "Judeo-Christian." In order to correct these potentially dangerous errors and misunderstandings, a more attentive study of the Greek and, especially, Hellenistic and neo-Platonic philosophical sources can be most helpful.

For Chrysippus all human beings constitute a single natural community,[95] and from this concept springs the humanitarian spirit of the Stoics. The Stoics reject the concept of hereditary nobility,[96] and the discussions of the humanists of the Quattrocento on this theme are inspired by the Stoic tradition, and these discussions are valid and important, but they are not original. The scholars of Renaissance humanism, myself included, have often found themselves in the strange position of attributing to the humanists certain original ideas that are then recognized as quotations from ancient authors. It is true that every theoretical affirmation, even when it is a reiteration or indeed a quotation from previous authors, has a direct validity as the reaffirmation of an important thought in a new context and often with new nuances, but the fact that it is a quotation or at least an imitation should not be ignored or forgotten. We might say in these cases as in many others that the originality of an author increases with the ignorance of his readers and interpreters, a ratio that obtains as well in many contemporary discussions.

Chrysippus also says that no man is a slave by nature,[97] and here we have the first philosophical doctrine, unanticipated by

95. Arnim 3, fr. 340ff.
96. Arnim 3, fr. 349ff.
97. Arnim 3, fr. 351–353.

Plato or Aristotle, that removed the theoretical foundation from the ancient institution of slavery. The fact that it took many centuries to abolish slavery does not diminish the merit of those thinkers who with their theory anticipated its practical application in much later times. If and to what point the ancient and modern adversaries of slavery were influenced by Stoic doctrine should be investigated.

On the other hand, Chrysippus does not recognize any moral bond between men and the other animals. Animals and the other irrational beings exist only for the advantage of men and of the gods, and only men and the gods constitute a true society and community.[98] The recent movement promoting animal rights finds no support in the doctrine of the Stoa or of other philosophical schools. We too oppose cruelty to animals, but as animals are not rational and have no juridical status, it seems to me more just to speak of the obligations of men toward animals, rather than of the rights of the animals themselves. But this does not suit the current climate where there is much talk of rights, especially those of one's own group, but rarely of obligations, ignoring the rule set down by Hobbes, not exactly a follower of natural law, that there is no right without a corresponding obligation.

Following Zeno, Chrysippus defines passion as excessive appetite,[99] but he considers all passions as judgments and distortions of the rational soul.[100] Passions are mistaken judgments (e.g., avarice is the opinion that wealth is a moral good).[101] Chrysippus distinguishes with Zeno four principal passions, but adds many subdivisions as he had also done for

98. Arnim 3, fr. 367ff.
99. Arnim 3, fr. 377ff.
100. Arnim 3, fr. 380ff., 456ff.
101. Arnim 3, fr. 456.

the virtues.[102] He then adds a very interesting and influential theory that the majority of historians have ignored: aside from the four bad passions, there are three good passions—joy, caution, and will—that correspond to three of the bad ones.[103] This doctrine is attested by Cicero and by other authors and is discussed by St. Augustine, by many medieval authors, and was even adopted by Spinoza.

The bad passions are to be eliminated, not simply moderated, and the wise man must be completely free from all passions.[104] On this point Stoic doctrine sets itself clearly apart from the teaching of the Peripatetics, who favor moderation and not the complete eradication of the passions.

Like Zeno, Chrysippus also distinguishes between good actions and suitable actions (*kathekonta*), he too insisting that these last have only a medium status and not one of being good.[105] The man who progresses toward wisdom performs all the suitable actions, but does not yet reach happiness. He does so only when the medium actions acquire a firm and habitual status.[106] All good actions are equal, and the same goes for all bad actions.[107] There is nothing in between virtue and vice.[108] Those who are near virtue are no less bad than those far from it, just as a person near the surface of the water drowns the same way as a person farther below.[109] The man who is progressing toward wisdom still does and says many

102. Arnim 3, fr. 387ff.
103. Arnim 3, fr. 431ff.
104. Arnim 3, fr. 443ff.
105. Arnim 3, fr. 494.
106. Arnim 3, fr. 510.
107. Arnim 3, fr. 527, 529.
108. Arnim 3, fr. 536.
109. Arnim 3, fr. 539.

bad things and must accept the blame for them.[110] But the man who reaches the status of the wise man does not realize it immediately.[111]

Chrysippus approves all the paradoxes proposed by Zeno,[112] but he admits that with their excessive grandeur and beauty they seem like fictions above the reach of human nature.[113] The wise man is never mistaken and always acts for the good.[114] He feels no pain, or to be more precise, when the wise man is tortured his body feels pain, but his soul does not surrender.[115] Therefore, the wise man is always happy, even in the bull of Phalaris[116] (here Chrysippus repeats the example given by Epicurus). Only the wise man is rich, beautiful, free, a prophet, pious, divine, a statesman, king, and legislator.[117] Wise men always agree with and help one another even without knowing each other.[118] The wise man is also a poet, orator, dialectician, and critic.[119] The wise man may love,[120] but he is never drunk.[121] He must not express himself with irony,[122] and he must not feel compassion.[123] Evidently in response to a doubt of Arcesilaus, Chrysippus maintains that the wise

110. Arnim 3, fr. 543.
111. Arnim 3, fr. 539ff.
112. Arnim 3, fr. 544.
113. Arnim 3, fr. 545.
114. Arnim 3, fr. 548ff., 557ff.
115. Arnim 3, fr. 567ff., 574.
116. Arnim 3, fr. 586.
117. Arnim 3, fr. 589–624.
118. Arnim 3, fr. 627.
119. Arnim 3, fr. 654.
120. Arnim 3, fr. 650ff.
121. Arnim 3, fr. 643–644.
122. Arnim 3, fr. 630.
123. Arnim 3, fr. 641.

man is recognized as such by perception on the basis of his form and appearance.[124] The critics also say the Stoic wise man has yet to be found anywhere, and that Chrysippus never said he himself or his predecessors were really wise men.[125]

Finally (and notable here is the doctrine of things indifferent but preferable), the wise man may pursue his financial advantage, participate in political life, and live at the court of kings or other governors.[126] Here we have a philosophical justification of the practical and active life that explains the great influence that Stoic thinkers had in the Greek and Roman political world.

Another philosophical doctrine that distinguishes the Stoics from other philosophical schools and also from Christian doctrine was their tendency to justify suicide.[127]

Stoic doctrine as it had been outlined by Zeno and then developed by Chrysippus was transmitted for many centuries in the Stoa of Athens, and also in other centers like Alexandria and Rome, and despite certain modifications it maintained a nucleus of orthodoxy. It was taken seriously by the rival schools, and a part of its doctrine has been preserved for us in the writings of its critics. Stoic concepts influenced and modified also the doctrine of the rival schools, especially the later phase of the Platonic Academy, and in the writings of Middle Platonism, of Philo, of the Church Fathers, and of the neo-Platonists we find many concepts of Stoic origin that were combined with elements that were new or of different origin and that have as a result often been ignored by historians. Especially,

124. Arnim 3, fr. 568.

125. Arnim 3, fr. 662, 668. See also Diogenes of Babylon (Arnim 3, fr. 32, pp. 216–17, Sextus Empiricus, *Adversus mathematicos* 9.133).

126. Arnim 3, fr. 685–700.

127. Arnim 3, fr. 757–768.

Stoic ethics with its ideal of the wise man and with its rigid concept of moral virtue free of pleasure, the passions, and external goods served as a model for many centuries down to modern times. It has elements in common with the doctrine of the Cynics that Zeno himself used, but it has a much stronger intellectual foundation and is more easily adaptable to the real conditions of practical life. The Stoic ideal has helped many people in various times to tolerate the evils and the vicissitudes of life. Thanks to the theory of things morally indifferent, the Stoic philosopher could follow without hesitation the ordinary affairs of life while being detached at the same time, since he knew that external things are not really good. Stoic physics gave to the philosopher the conviction that his moral ideal was a part of the universal order of nature with which he had to align himself through his moral efforts. The moral end, though it might be reached by few, or perhaps by none, was proposed to all men by nature itself; and thus they arrived at a humane and humanitarian attitude that embraced the whole of humankind. The doctrine of natural law, based on the postulate of a fundamental harmony between human justice and the reason or law of the whole world, was a lasting inspiration in the history of juridical and political thought in the Western world. Stoic logic as developed by Chrysippus served as an effective instrument to refute the school's critics and their arguments, and was a necessity for those who had faith in the power of rational discourse and were not merely satisfied by edifying sermons. The allegorical interpretation of popular religion led to a single or at least supreme eternal God who was at the same time the principle of nature and the source of moral principles, a concept that would please Philo and many Christian writers of the early centuries. Outside of Platonism, Stoicism was their most important source as they attempted to construct out of the historical, legal, and moral elements of the Bible a cosmological and theological system with the aid of Greek culture and philosophy to the extent that it was compatible with the central teachings of the Jewish and Christian religions.

Medieval philosophy from the twelfth century on was dominated by Aristotelian doctrine, but it includes as well many neo-Platonic and also Stoic elements transmitted by the Roman and Christian authors of late Antiquity. Latin philosophical terminology, developed after the Greek model by Roman authors and later by the Scholastics, includes many terms of Stoic origin and thus reflects the influence of Stoic doctrine, and it has often served as the basis for the philosophical terminology of the modern languages. Despite the transformations due to the new philosophical and scientific ideas of recent centuries, the ancient sources of our so-called ordinary discourse are easily recognized when we study the origin and history of the abstract terms that we are accustomed to using. Stoic thought was often taken up by the humanists and thinkers of the Renaissance, and many of their ideas which at first glance seem new and original are in reality ancient and often Stoic doctrines transmitted by Cicero, Seneca, or others, with slight and frequently interesting modifications. Petrarch, Poggio, and Pomponazzi come to mind as examples. With Lipsius and some thinkers of the seventeenth century we note an actual rebirth of Stoicism, based not only on the well-known Roman writers but in part on the scattered Greek testimonies that have been systematically collected only in our century by Arnim. Stoic influences are noted as well in the ethics of Spinoza and of Kant and of many more recent thinkers.

I take the liberty now of ending with an observation that may not please many people, but that I feel must be made. In recent discussions it is often held that a moral, philosophical, or religious end cannot be valid if it cannot be reached by the majority of people. In agreement with the Stoics and Kant, but also with many serious theologians, I should like to turn that argument on its head: a moral end that is not reached by the majority of people, for that very fact becomes more valid, and no less true. Human beings, on the whole or for the most part, have a very imperfect life. If we accept this fact as normal, it means that we are approving of imperfection and making life worse than it already is. An end that is not easily or completely attainable at least stimulates our efforts toward a more perfect life than the present one. I would like to conclude with a saying of Goethe: We must aim for the impossible in order to reach the possible.

CHAPTER FIVE

Carneades and
Philo of Larissa

We have seen how the Stoic doctrine of Zeno was criticized by
Arcesilaus, head of the Second Academy, who had replaced
the "dogmatic" doctrine of the first successors of Plato with a
Skeptic doctrine influenced by Pyrrho. We have also seen how
Chrysippus, the second successor of Zeno, elaborating and
consolidating the Stoic doctrine, tried to refute the skeptical
objections of Arcesilaus, especially those concerning the theory of knowledge and the criterion of truth. Chrysippus' doctrine dominated almost all the successive tradition of Stoicism,
but it had to confront a new attack from the Academic school.

The spokesman for that criticism was Carneades, head of the so-called Third Academy.

Carneades of Cyrene, who lived circa 213 to 128 B.C., was the student of the Academic Hegesippus and also of the Stoic Diogenes of Babylon, second successor of Chrysippus as head of the Stoa. Carneades became head of the Academy in 160. He had a profound knowledge of the philosophical doctrines of all the schools and distinguished himself for his dialectical acumen as well as for his eloquence. Primarily he sought to criticize the doctrine of Chrysippus, whose writings he knew in detail. Cleverly modifying the popular saying that if it were not for Chrysippus, there would be no Stoa, Carneades said of himself: If it were not for Chrysippus, I would not be either.[1] In 156 Carneades, together with his teacher Diogenes and with other heads of the schools of philosophy, was part of an Athenian embassy to Rome.[2] This episode was important for the introduction of Greek philosophy to Rome, and we know that the discourses delivered by Carneades in Rome made a profound impression on his listeners.

Like Arcesilaus, Carneades diffused his doctrines by means of teaching, but left no published writings. We know the thought of Carneades primarily through the writings of his disciple Clitomachus of Carthage,[3] whose writings have them-

---

1. Diogenes Laertius, *Vitae et Placita philosophorum* 4.62; *Karneades: Fragmente, Text und Kommentar,* ed. B. Wiśniewski, fr. 1.

2. Cicero, *Tusculanae Disputationes* 4.5; Wiśniewski, fr. 4.

3. Clitomachus is repeatedly quoted by Cicero (*Academica Priora* 78, 98, 102, 108, 137, 139; *De divinatione* 2.87) and was probably the principal source for what Cicero says about the doctrine of Carneades, especially in the *Acad. Pr.* (64–139). See Sextus Empiricus, *Adversus mathematicos* 9.182.

selves been lost. Clitomachus lived from 186 to 109 B.C. and was the successor of Carneades and head of the Academy from 128 until his death. On all essential points, he was a faithful follower of his teacher, and thanks to Clitomachus, as read and quoted by Cicero and Sextus Empiricus, we are much better informed on the doctrine of Carneades than on that of Pyrrho or Arcesilaus. It seems that Clitomachus was Cicero's principal source for entire sections of his writings, especially in the *Academica Priora* and *Posteriora*, *De natura deorum*, *De divinatione*, and *De fato* (but not in the *De finibus*).

Carneades on many points took up the doctrine of Arcesilaus, and he too criticized the Stoics, but he did not limit his criticism to the Stoics alone.[4] His main argument against the criterion of truth is more general and more comprehensive than that of his predecessor. There is no criterion of truth, neither the intellect (*logos*), nor perception, nor phantasy, nor any other thing, because all these things deceive us.[5] In another argument Carneades maintains that the evident phantasy that indicates itself and the phenomenon that produces it cannot be a sure criterion, as Epicurus believed, since phantasy is often different from its objects and hence can deceive us.[6]

Another argument directed by Carneades against the Stoics resembles one by Arcesilaus but is more precise: There is no true phantasy that could not also be false, and for every phantasy that seems real a false phantasy can be found that is indistinguishable from it. Hence, there is no comprehending

4. Sext. Emp. 7.159; Wiśniewski, fr. 76.
5. Wiśniewski, fr. 76.
6. Sext. Emp. 7.160–63; Wiśniewski, fr. 76.

(*kataleptike*) phantasy that can serve as a sure criterion of truth. Also, reasoning is no solid criterion (and this is true also for the Platonists and the Peripatetics) because it is based on perception and phantasy.[7] In the anti-Stoic part of his argument, Carneades insists on the indistinguishability (*aparallaxia*) between phantasies derived from existing and nonexistent things and cites as examples the likeness between our normal perceptions and those that happen in dreams or in a state of madness. Hence, false phantasies no less than true ones lead us to assent and to the actions that come from assent, and we cannot distinguish between the comprehending phantasies and the non-comprehending ones. Carneades cites also other examples of things different but indistinguishable, like twin brothers or two eggs.[8] Here we have in an implicit form the principle of complete individualization, which was to have a long history until Leibniz.

Carneades also uses various sophisms, like the one of the veiled person whose identity cannot be recognized, of the round tower that seems flat from afar, of the straight stick that seems broken in the water, and of the shores that seem to move as we pass them by ship. The sophism of the Sorites had already been used by Arcesilaus to cast doubt on the distinction between the comprehending and non-comprehending phantasy. Chrysippus had replied (not too convincingly) that the wise man, when he faces such questions from his adversaries, should stop and refuse to go on, remaining tranquil.[9] Carneades pushes on and retorts (not without irony): As far as I am concerned, let the wise man stay tranquil and

---

7. Sext. Emp. 7.164–65; Wiśniewski, fr. 76.

8. Sext. Emp. 7.402–21; Wiśniewski, fr. 79.

9. Wiśniewski, fr. 79. See Cic., *Acad. Pr.* 79ff.

even start snoring, but it does not help him, because someone will always be there to wake him up and ask him the same question.[10]

Carneades even doubts the certainty of the axioms in mathematics and of its method of demonstration and holds that mathematicians cannot even take one step forward unless they are granted their axioms.[11] In natural philosophy there is still less certainty, since the philosophers do not agree with each other.[12]

We know one argument that Carneades used against Stoic theology. If the world is an animal, also the gods are animals, hence they have perception and the five senses, they feel pleasure and pain, and are corruptible, therefore they do not exist.[13] If Zeus is a god, the day, the month, and the year are gods too. Carneades uses a whole series of such Sorites to refute the Stoic doctrine of the existence of the gods.[14] Another argument parodies Zeno: To be literate is better than not to be literate. There is nothing better than the world. Therefore the world is literate, and for the same reason the world must be eloquent, a mathematician, musician, learned in all forms of knowledge, and finally a philosopher.[15]

We also know some of his arguments that place divination in doubt and are aimed particularly at the Stoics. There is no

10. Cic., *Acad. Pr.* 93; Wiśniewski, fr. 88.

11. Galen, *De optima doctrina* 2.45; Wisniewski, fr. 85; see Cic., *Acad. Pr.* 116.

12. Cic., *Acad. Pr.* 117.

13. Sext. Emp. 9.138–41; Wisniewski, fr. 93.

14. Sext. Emp. 9.182–90; Wisniewski, fr. 93; see Cicero, *De natura deorum* 3.43–44; Wisniewski, fr. 95.

15. Cic., *De nat. deorum* 3.22–23.

divination for objects of the senses, of the arts and sciences, of philosophy and of politics.[16] Also some arguments against astrology can be attributed to Carneades.[17]

Chrysippus had defended the deterministic doctrine of fate and had tried to leave space for free will by introducing the concept of concurrent causes (*confatalia*) that together produce their effects. Carneades completely rejects Stoic determinism. If everything follows from preceding causes, necessity determines everything, and nothing depends on us. But something does depend on us, and hence not everything depends on fate.[18] Carneades also criticized the doctrine of Epicurus on the deviation of atoms, saying that free will could be defended also without using this completely fictitious theory.[19]

Carneades also treated ethical problems after his fashion. He insists on the discrepancy among various philosophers on the theory of good and evil,[20] but he concedes that the difference between the Stoics and the Peripatetics on this issue is more verbal than real.[21] Carneades also affirmed that fame was desirable, and he forced the later Stoics to accept this doctrine.[22]

As for the supreme good, Carneades presented a scheme of the possible opinions and defined the moral end (perhaps only

16. Cic., *De div.* 2.9–12; Wiśniewski, fr. 99.

17. E. Zeller, *Die Philosophie der Griechen*, ed. E. Wellmann, 3:1.530*n*4, quoting A. Schmekel, *Die Philosophie der mittleren Stoa in ihrem geschichtlichen Zusammenhang dargestellt*, pp. 155–84, with references to Sextus Empiricus, Gellius, and St. Augustine.

18. Cicero, *De fato* 31; Wiśniewski, fr. 103.

19. Cic., *De fato* 23; Wiśniewski, fr. 104.

20. Cic., *Acad. Pr.* 129–31.

21. Cicero, *De finibus* 3.41; Wiśniewski, fr. 135.

22. Cic., *De fin.* 3.57; Wiśniewski, fr. 157.

hypothetically) as the enjoyment of the things that are first according to nature—that is, health, beauty, and the absence of pain.[23] Here too he is criticizing Stoic doctrine, which defines the end and the supreme good as identical with virtue alone.[24]

Up to this point we have described Carneades only as the successor of Arcesilaus, namely as a Skeptic and critic of the dogmatic schools, and especially of the Stoic doctrine of Chrysippus. But unlike Arcesilaus and the other pure Skeptics, Carneades introduced some important modifications in Skeptic doctrine, and this explains why historical tradition treats Carneades not as a simple follower and successor of Arcesilaus, but as the head and founder of a new Third Academy.[25] Carneades was perhaps the first to introduce into logical and philosophical discourse the concept of the probable (*pithanon*), which stands in the middle between the certain and the dubious. The New Academy was therefore characterized by probabilism, especially in the ethical discussion about good and evil. He holds that what is said about good and about evil is more probable than the opposite opinion. Carneades contrasts the probable to the improbable and then distinguishes three levels of probable phantasies: some phantasies are simply probable, others are probable and also examined, and still others are probable and examined and not contradicted. Carneades uses as an example of the probable examined phantasy a serpent in a dark house that turns out to be a rope, and as the example of a dubious phantasy the presence of Alcestis,

23. Cic., *De fin.* 5.16–21. See also *De fin.* 2.35, 38, 42; 4.49; *Acad. Pr.* 131; Wiśniewski, fr. 133, 134, 141, 144, 146.

24. Cic., *Tusc.* 5.83; Wiśniewski, fr. 132.

25. Sextus Empiricus, *Pyrrhonianae Dissertationes* 1.220; Eusebius, *Praeparatio Evangelica* 14.7; Wiśniewski, fr. 18, 31.

which at least at first is contradicted by the knowledge of her death. Despite the fact that everything is uncertain, for Carneades the probable is sufficient for judging and acting in daily life.[26] Carneades, while denying phantasies as certain, does admit different levels of probable phantasies and accepts the most probable ones as a criterion, at least for the evaluations and actions of daily life.

According to other testimonies, phantasy has two points of reference—the object from which it comes, and the subject in which it is found. With respect to its object a phantasy is true or false; with respect to its subject the phantasy is called apparently true or apparently false. The apparently true phantasy is called appearance (*emphasis*) or probability or probable phantasy, and the apparently false one is called non-appearance (*apemphasis*) or improbability or improbable phantasy. What immediately appears false cannot persuade us, nor what is true but does not appear true. An obviously false phantasy cannot serve as a criterion, as, for example, the representation of Electra in the insane mind of Orestes. An apparently true phantasy can be either weak or strong. The weak phantasy is of no use as a criterion. Instead the apparently true phantasy that carries sufficient force is the criterion of truth for Carneades.[27] According to this testimony, Carneades formulated a criterion for truth different from that of Arcesilaus, and this criterion falls within the limits of his probabilism and hence is much less strong and decisive than the Stoic criterion. There are also various levels of the probable and of this criterion. An apparently true phantasy can be really true or false, but as it is probable it can serve as a criterion; we must follow it since it is

26. Sext. Emp., *Pyrrh. Diss.* 1.226–31, and *Adv. math.* 7.166; see Wiśniewski, fr. 127, 129.

27. Sext. Emp., *Adv. math.* 7.167–73; Wiśiewski, fr. 129.

rarely false and usually true, because we must regulate our decisions and actions on the basis of what is true in the majority of cases, and this is the common and first criterion according to Carneades. The second criterion, which seems even stronger, is the probable and uncontradicted phantasy. For example, we see a man and we observe that he has all the external and internal qualities of Socrates. So we think it is Socrates since he has all his usual qualities and there is no other person indistinguishable from him. Thus, as a doctor judges the sickness of a patient according to the combination of all symptoms, the Academic philosopher arrives at a judgment of truth according to the combination of all phantasies. Still more perfect is the examined phantasy in which every facet has been verified. We regulate ourselves in everything on the basis of probable phantasies. Simply probable phantasies are enough for minor questions, and they must suffice when there is little time to deliberate. For important decisions we follow the uncontradicted phantasies, and in those things that concern happiness we follow the examined phantasies, as also with important decisions when we have enough time to deliberate.[28]

We note between this presentation and the previous one a terminological discrepancy. In the first discourse examined phantasy occupies the second place and uncontradicted phantasy the third and most perfect place. In the second discourse this order is reversed, and the second level is called uncontradicted and the third and most perfect is called examined. It is not probable that Carneades himself changed his mind on this important point. It seems more probable to me that one of our two sources made an error. And I am more inclined to think that the second version, which treats examined phan-

28. Sext. Emp., *Adv. math.* 7.74–189; Wiśniewski, fr. 129.

tasy as the third and most perfect criterion, is more probable and closer to the authentic thought of Carneades.

Another less clear formulation is to be found in Cicero. In our phantasies (*visa*) we must make two distinctions. There are those that can be perceived and others that cannot. Then there are probable and improbable phantasies. That which is said against the senses and against their evidence (*perspicuitas*) belongs to the first division (between things that can or cannot be perceived). Nothing ought to be said against the second division (between probable and improbable phantasies). It follows that there is no phantasy such that we can infer from it the perception of an object; instead there are many phantasies that are probable. The wise man follows the probable (since he has not the possibility of following the certain).[29] The Academics distinguish between things probable and improbable. But that is not enough to affirm that some things can be perceived (as certain) or not—because many false things are probable, but nothing false can be perceived or known. Therefore, those are mistaken who believe that the Academics deny the senses; the Academics never deny color or taste or sound, they only doubt that these sensations contain a proper criterion (*nota*) of the true and certain.[30] There follows an interesting discourse on the sense in which Carneades understands the suspension of judgment. When he says that the wise man must suspend his assent, this assertion is to be taken in two different senses. In the first sense it is . . . affirmed that the wise man must never give his assent. In the second sense it is understood that every time a probability happens or does not happen the wise man follows this probability and may respond or not respond. However, the wise man does not ap-

29. Cic., *Acad. Pr.* 99; Wiśniewski, fr. 126.
30. Cic., *Acad. Pr.* 103.

prove all the phantasies of this type, but only those that are not hindered (that is, contradicted) by anything.[31] Here we see that Carneades maintains the Skeptic position in the episte- mological sense and insists that in a theoretical sense nothing should be confirmed as certain, but that in practical situations we may follow the probable without making any theoretical assertion. Still, according to Cicero, Carneades denies assent— that is, opinion and temerity—but he does not renounce ac- tion, following the probable not contradicted by anything.[32] Also the principle that nothing can be known is not known with certainty, but merely probable,[33] and therefore the Skep- tic position is not refuted by itself, as its adversaries claim. Cicero says several times that Carneades at times concedes that the wise man may have opinions, but he quotes Clito- machus at one point, who asserted that Carneades made this concession only in the context of his discussion and not in a definitive sense.[34]

Another aspect of the doctrine of Carneades is found in Eusebius. Like Arcesilaus, Carneades also used as a method the arguments that lead to opposite conclusions, refuting the doctrines of the other philosophers, but he parts ways with Arcesilaus in his doctrine of suspension. One must distinguish between the incomprehensible and the uncertain. All things are incomprehensible, but not all are uncertain—that is, there is no true knowledge according to the criterion of the Stoics, but we can conduct ourselves in life according to what is uncertain but probable. So it is said (with a slightly critical and

---

31. Cic., *Acad. Pr.* 104 (see also 33); Wiśniewski, fr. 128.

32. Cic., *Acad. Pr.* 108; Wiśniewski, fr. 108.

33. Cic., *Acad. Pr.* 109–10; Wiśniewski, fr. 117.

34. Cic., *Acad. Pr.* 78 (see also 59, 67, 112); Wiśniewski, fr. 109, 111–113.

polemical tone) that Carneades was not concerned with truth but only with what seems probable to common people. Still, according to Eusebius, Carneades concedes that true and false are present in things themselves and that they are both present according to the weight of probability, but neither of the two can be comprehended in a sure way—because true and false phantasies are often similar to one another (as in the case of a real egg and a wax egg, which are often indistinguishable).[35]

There remain some uncertainties in the tradition on Carneades, but I do not think the opinions attributed to him are only dialectical arguments he did not take seriously. We also know that Carneades was criticized by his contemporary, the Stoic Antipater of Tarsus, but the arguments of Antipater were rebutted by Carneades himself.[36]

Carneades' influence was notable, especially on Panaetius who modified Stoic doctrine to respond to the criticism of Carneades, and then on Cicero who quotes Clitomachus and was the direct pupil of two other Academics, Philo and Antiochus, and even on Sextus Empiricus who criticized Carneades for his less radical version of Skepticism, but seemingly derived many anti-Stoic arguments from him.

In the history of Skepticism Carneades formulated a less extreme position called probabilism, and this position constitutes an independent and intermediate doctrine between radical Skepticism and the dogmatism of the other schools. The position of probabilism has been taken up subsequently in various epochs and has found many followers in our century, as much among the physicists and mathematicians who must take account of serious changes in the observations and theo-

35. Eus., *Praep. Evang.* 14.7–8.
36. Cic., *Acad. Pr.* 28; Wiśniewski, fr. 116.

ries on which they base themselves as among the theoreticians and philosophers opposed to rationalistic thought and to historical and philological evidence and dedicated to the legal and political reasoning in which the method of the rhetoricians and of the sophists seems more valid and useful than logical, philosophical, philological, or historical precision.

The Skeptic period of the Academic school ends with Philo of Larissa, who lived from 159 to 79 B.C. and was the student of Clitomachus and his successor as head of the Academy from 109. Philo followed the Skeptic-probabilistic theory of Carneades and Clitomachus during the first phase of his career, but in a subsequent phase he moved to a more dogmatic position under the influence of his student, Antiochus of Ascalon, but in a far less decisive fashion than Antiochus. For his intermediate position between the Skepticism of Carneades and the dogmatism of Antiochus, he is sometimes called the founder of a Fourth Academy.[37] He was in Rome in 88 B.C. and was one of the principal teachers of Cicero. The widespread opinion that Cicero was a Stoic philosopher is based on confusion and is completely erroneous, and I am sorry that I even have to mention it. In his dialogues Cicero presented orthodox Stoic doctrine but never as the doctrine he approved, and usually he follows it with a rebuttal of Academic tendency. The most that can be said on the subject is that Cicero presents orthodox Stoic doctrine with more sympathy than that of Epicurus. The doctrine that he approves is always the Academic doctrine of his teachers, namely the Skeptic doctrine of Philo or the dogmatic doctrine of Antiochus. The only work in which Cicero presents Stoic doctrine as his own is the *De officiis*, and here he does not follow the orthodox doctrine of the Stoic school, but rather the modified version of Panaetius.

37. Sext. Emp., *Pyrrh. Diss.* 1.220.

The philosophical position of Cicero was not Stoic but Academic and in part Skeptic, in part eclectic.

Our information on Philo of Larissa is scarce and must be used with caution since we know that he changed his doctrine during the course of his own career. We know for sure that at first he followed Carneades and Clitomachus. The Skeptic position expounded by Cicero in the *Academica Posteriora* is surely based on the spoken teaching, if not on the writings of Philo, as Cicero himself states in one of his letters.[38] But Cicero quotes Clitomachus as his principal source, and it seems difficult to reconstruct the Skepticism of Philo since none of the Skeptic arguments presented by Cicero and not identified with Carneades are clearly attributed to Philo.

We are better informed on the later and semidogmatic position of Philo. We learn from Sextus Empiricus that according to Philo things are incomprehensible in the sense of the Stoic criterion of the comprehending phantasy, but that according to the nature of the things themselves they are comprehensible.[39] In other words, Philo continued to reject the Stoic criterion of the comprehending phantasy and to keep up the polemic against it, but he went beyond the probabilism of Carneades and moved to a form of dogmatism. It seems this change of position is due to the fact that Philo, while denying the Stoic criterion, was not willing to draw the consequence that there is no difference between what is known and what is unknown. According to Eusebius, it was the evidence and consistency of our experiences that pushed him to abandon the principle that nothing can be comprehended.[40] Cicero as well, following Antiochus, offers a similar explanation. Philo

38. Cicero, *Epistolae ad Familiares* 9.8: mihi sumpsi Philonis.
39. Sext. Emp., *Pyrrh. Diss.* 1.235.
40. Eus., *Praep. Evang.* 14.9.

denied that anything could be comprehended in the sense of comprehension as defined by Zeno, but he did not want to abandon the distinction between the unknown and the known, and hence he abandoned the Skeptic position that nothing can be known.[41] He tried to give to the doctrine of Carneades a more positive and less Skeptic interpretation than the one offered by Clitomachus. According to Philo, it is permissible to say with Carneades that we cannot comprehend or perceive anything, but that we can nonetheless have opinions on the basis of what Carneades calls probable.[42] We find also other traces of an interpretation given to Carneades by Philo and different from that of Clitomachus.

We know an argument used by Philo against Antiochus. Antiochus had criticized the anti-Stoic argument of Philo (and of Carneades) that false phantasies are not distinguishable from true ones, since that presupposes that there are false phantasies. Philo responds that he was not denying the difference between true and false, but that he treated it as probable and that he was not accepting any valid criterion for their comprehension or objective distinction.[43]

Philo also tried to justify his philosophical position with a historical interpretation of Academic doctrine. He tried in a way that was considered new to harmonize the Old and the New Academy. He denied both in his teaching and in his writings that there were two different Academies and that the position of the Academy was Skeptic.[44] It appears then that Philo returned to the Old Academy and tried to move the doctrine of the New Academy closer to that of the Old, insist-

41. Cic., *Acad. Pr.* 18.

42. Cic., *Acad. Pr.* 78.

43. Cic., *Acad. Pr.* 111.

44. Cic., *Acad. Pr.* 12; Cicero, *Academica Posteriora* 13.

ing on the positive aspect in the thought of Carneades, while on the other hand keeping up his polemic against the Stoics and especially against their criterion of truth. Even the report, probably false, that we find in Sextus, Diogenes Laertius, and Eusebius and that presents Arcesilaus as a secretly dogmatic thinker I think stems from Philo.

Another doctrine of Philo is attested by Stobaeus. It is on the division of ethics and uses the analogy between philosophy and medicine, a theme we have already come across a few times. The first part of ethics is protreptic and directs the student toward philosophy. The second part is therapeutic and treats of goods and evils. The third part treats of the ends and of the happiness that corresponds with the body's health. The fourth part deals with the various forms of human life, including politics. The last three parts would be sufficient if all men were wise, but since many men are of a mediocre disposition, the protreptic part is also necessary.[45] Here we have a doctrine that sounds dogmatic, but contains no element of Stoicism.

There are many passages in Cicero that I would be inclined to attribute to Philo, without being completely sure. In the *De finibus* Cicero attacks the criterion of the Stoics as well as their doctrine that virtue alone is sufficient for happiness, preferring the Peripatetic doctrine (which recognizes external goods as goods and as components of happiness).[46] Elsewhere Cicero criticizes the Stoics on the same point, approves the doctrine of the Old Academy and of the Peripatetic school (which is essentially the same), and criticizes Zeno for having abandoned the consensus of the two previous schools.[47] This posi-

---

45. Stobaeus, *Eclogae*, 2.7.2.
46. Cic., *De fin.* 5.76–78.
47. Cic., *De fin.* 4.3–4, 19, 44–45, 57, 60, 72.

tion, favorable to the Old Academy and to the Peripatetic school but hostile to the Stoics, seems to reflect the attitude of Philo. Also, another passage in Cicero—where he argues against Epicurus that pleasure and the absence of pain are not identical and where the early Academics and Peripatetics are cited—may stem from Philo rather than from Carneades, who is mentioned but also criticized.[48]

I would be inclined to characterize the position of Philo not only as semidogmatic but also as eclectic. He continues, like his Skeptic predecessors Arcesilaus and Carneades, with the anti-Stoic polemic, but he insists on a fundamental agreement between the Old Academy and the Peripatetic school. Another notable fact, important and significant in a teacher of Cicero, is that Philo, unlike the majority of his predecessors and successors in the Academy, approved and taught rhetoric as a part of philosophy, following on this point the example of Aristotle and his school.[49]

The position of Philo as we have tried to describe it, though not without some hesitation, explains both the position of Cicero who follows him on many points and that of Antiochus who went a step further: he completely abandoned the Skepticism of Arcesilaus, Carneades, and Philo, even forsaking their anti-Stoic polemic, and returned to an open dogmatism, proclaiming that he was renewing the doctrine of the Old Academy, but modifying it with doctrines taken from the Peripatetics and Stoics, and even with some new and original doctrines.

48. Cic., *De fin.* 2.9ff., 34ff., 42ff.
49. Cic., *Tusc.* 2.9; Cicero, *De oratore* 3.110.

CHAPTER SIX

Panaetius

After Chrysippus' death the orthodox Stoic doctrine was carried on by several of his successors, but toward the middle of the second century B.C. it was changed on several important points, first by Panaetius and then by Posidonius. This was due in part to new ideas, in part to attempts to refute the critical arguments used by Carneades against the doctrine of Chrysippus. But also noticeable is a tendency to accept some elements of Platonic and Aristotelian philosophy and to harmonize them with the orthodox doctrine of the Stoic school. For this reason, the ancient sources distinguish the later Stoics from the early Stoics, and modern scholars speak of Middle Stoicism as distinct from the Ancient Stoicism of Zeno and

Chrysippus and from the New Stoicism of Seneca, Epictetus, and Marcus Aurelius.

Middle Stoicism offers the first example of the kind of eclecticism that would emerge in the Fourth and Fifth Academies and in the philosophical writings of Cicero, who was their disciple, and that dominated the entire philosophical literature until the third century A.D.—that is, until Plotinus.

Panaetius, his student Posidonius, and the Academic Antiochus of Ascalon constitute the trio of great unknown thinkers to whom modern historians, for good and at times for bad reasons, have attributed all the new ideas and all the combinations of new and old ideas missing from the earlier traditions of the different schools. These innovations appear for the first time in the writings of authors like Cicero, Seneca, or Albinus, writers who are anything but original, but who preserve for us the ideas of their teachers and predecessors whose writings we do not have. The sources and direct testimonies are rather scarce, and many reconstructions and attributions, including some I myself have suggested or defended, are rather hypothetical or uncertain. In some cases one notes the tendency to attribute to a thinker the entire content of certain books of Cicero when he quotes the author only a few times and on very specific doctrines. We shall try to pursue a middle way, keeping to the obvious or probable attributions and renouncing theories that are either too ambitious or without sufficient foundation.

Panaetius was born in Rhodes of a noble family circa 185 B.C. He studied at Pergamon under the grammarian Crates of Mallos and then at Athens at the Stoa under Diogenes of Babylon and Antipater of Tarsus. He spent much time in Rome where he was active in the circle of Scipio Africanus the Younger whom he accompanied to the East in 141. He succeeded his teacher Antipater as head of the Stoic school in 128 and died toward 110. He had many disciples, of whom Posidonius was the most famous. For being a philosopher of Scipio's circle, through the content and style of his thought, and perhaps also through the influence of Diodotus (Cicero's private teacher), Panaetius was one of Cicero's favorite authors; Cicero quotes him often and uses him as his main source in the first two books of the *De officiis*. Outside of Cicero all we have are scattered notices, especially in Diogenes Laertius.

On many essential points Panaetius remained faithful to the Stoic tradition, while on others he introduced very significant changes. Aside from his personal preferences, two factors influenced his thought: Carneades' attack against the doctrine of Chrysippus, and Panaetius' direct knowledge of the writings of the Platonic and Aristotelian schools.

On several points Panaetius abandoned the Stoic position, yielding to the criticisms of Carneades, as we shall see. His preference for the ancient philosophers and for the leaders of the other schools is directly recorded; he admired Plato and Aristotle and abandoned several teachings of Zeno in favor of those of the Academy or of the Peripatetics.[1] We know that Panaetius advised a Roman student of his to learn by heart the book on mourning by the Academic Crantor.[2] Cicero informs us that Panaetius held Plato in special admiration and tried not to contradict him,[3] and that he would quote often and approvingly from Xenocrates, Aristotle, Theophrastus, and Dicaearchus.[4] So we may call him eclectic without using the word in a negative sense. Like his successors, Panaetius took

---

1. *Stoicorum Index Herculanensis*, col. 61; *Panaetii Rhodii Fragmenta*, ed. M. Van Straaten, fr. 57.

2. Cicero, *Academica Priora* 135; Van Straaten, fr. 137.

3. Cicero, *Tusculanae Disputationes* 1.79; Van Straaten, fr. 83.

4. Cicero, *De finibus* 4.79; Van Straaten, fr. 55.

the truth from all the sources available to him and not from the doctrines of a single school; his is an attitude that we find in many authors of late Antiquity as well as in much later thinkers (as, for example, in Giovanni Pico della Mirandola).

A thorough knowledge of the ancient authors and a strong grammatical and critical preparation explain some literary judgments attributed to Panaetius, which give credit to his competence as a philologist and historian. For example, he said that among the Socratic dialogues only those of Plato, Xenophon, Antisthenes, and Aeschines were authentic, while those of Phaedo and Euclid were doubtful, and the others apocryphal.[5] This testimony was probably the source for the tradition that Panaetius cast doubt on the authenticity of the *Phaedo* of Plato.[6] Panaetius maintains that the first book of the *Republic* was revised by Plato more than once,[7] he speaks of the writings of Ariston and Aristippus,[8] and he quotes a book by the latter on the philosophical sects that may have served as an important doxographical source for him and others.[9] He praises Xenophanes and Anaxagoras,[10] and he tries to identify Aristides.[11] He denies the story that Socrates was

5. Diogenes Laertius, *Vitae et Placita philosophorum* 2.64; Van Straaten, fr. 126.

6. Asclepius, *In Metaphysicam Aristotelis* 991b3; Elias, *In Categorias Aristotelis* 233 (quoting Syrianus); Van Straaten, fr. 127–129. Panaetius denied the immortality of the soul, and since the *Phaedo* defended it, he either had to criticize Plato or to consider the *Phaedo* as apocryphal (Asclepius, *In Metaphysicam*; Cic., *Tusc.* 1.79–80; Van Straaten, fr. 127 and 83).

7. Diog. Laert. 3.37; Van Straaten, fr. 130.

8. Diog. Laert. 7.163 and 2.85; Van Straaten, fr. 123 and 124.

9. Diog. Laert. 2.87; Van Straaten, fr. 49.

10. Diog. Laert. 9.20; Van Straaten, fr. 45.

11. Plutarch, *Aristides* 1.16; Van Straaten, fr. 131.

bigamous,[12] and examines a grammatical problem with passages taken from Plato.[13] He praises Demosthenes because in his speeches he presupposes that the moral good should be chosen for itself, and that the moral good and decorum are preferable to security and safety,[14] thus making him a Stoic philosopher *ante litteram.* He quotes the grammarian Aristarchus,[15] and it seems he wrote on the doctrine of Democritus as well.[16]

Moving from the historical and philological erudition of Panaetius to his philosophical doctrine, we see that he considers physics as the first part of philosophy[17] (unlike Chrysippus who gave first place to logic). We know little of his logic, but we do know that Panaetius accepted with Chrysippus the comprehending phantasy as the criterion of truth, but added under Carneades' influence that this phantasy must be uncontradicted, using also the examples of Helena and of Alcestis.[18] As for the physics of Panaetius, we know from several sources that he rejected the periodic destruction of the world taught by Chrysippus and accepted instead with Aristotle the eternity of the world.[19] He showed interest in astronomy[20] and proposed a definition of comets that distin-

12. Van Straaten, fr. 132–134.

13. Van Straaten, fr. 92.

14. Van Straaten, fr. 94.

15. Van Straaten, fr. 93.

16. Panaetius wrote a work entitled *Peri euthumias,* using a term preferred by Democritus (Diog. Laert. 9.20; Van Straaten, fr. 45).

17. Diog. Laert. 7.41; Van Straaten, fr. 63.

18. Sextus Empiricus, *Adversus mathematicos* 7.253–57; Van Straaten, fr. 91.

19. Van Straaten, fr. 64–69 (quoting Cicero, Philo of Alexandria, Diogenes Laertius, Arnobius, Epiphanius, and Stobaeus).

20. Cicero, *De re publica* 1.15; Van Straaten, fr. 77.

guishes them from other stars.[21] He affirms that, because of its climate, Attica produces many gifted people,[22] and that also the hot zone is inhabited.[23] The division between the religions of the politicians, the poets, and the philosophers proposed by Varro and attested by St. Augustine has often been attributed to Panaetius but may also go back to Posidonius.[24]

Panaetius wrote a treatise on providence,[25] but he denied divination in all its forms,[26] abandoning Chrysippus' doctrine also on this point and following Carneades. He particularly rejects the astrology of the Chaldeans, and the passage in Cicero's *De divinatione* that deals with this subject is clearly based on Panaetius.[27] Panaetius makes a distinction between reason and testimonies as the bases of an argument, following a rhetorical tradition that through Cicero and St. Augustine prepared the way for the medieval distinction between *ratio* and *auctoritas*. Arguing against astrology, Panaetius cites the case of twins born under the same constellation, insists on the almost infinite distances of the planets and the fixed stars, and asserts that the stars rise and set at different times according to the places from which they are observed, and that different persons are born at the same time. Outside of the stars, one has to consider the parents and the climate and admit that

21. Seneca, *Naturales quaestiones* 7.30.2; Van Straaten, fr. 75.

22. Proclus, *In Timaeum* 50b; Van Straaten, fr. 76.

23. Van Straaten, fr. 135.

24. Augustine, *The City of God* [*De civitate Dei*] 4.27. Van Straaten omits to mention this.

25. Cicero, *Epistolae ad Atticum* 13.8; Van Straaten, fr. 33.

26. Cic., *Acad. Pr.* 107; Cicero, *De divinatione* 1.6 and 1.12; Diog. Laert. 7.149; Van Straaten, fr. 70–73.

27. Cic., *De div.* 2.88–97; Van Straaten, fr. 74.

natural defects can be corrected by instruction and by medical cures.[28]

Our soul is material and consists of fire and air.[29] Of the eight parts of the soul that the Stoics talked about, Panaetius accepts only six (namely, the five senses and the governing part), and he rejects the faculty of speech, which belongs instead to motion, and the vegetative part, which belongs to nature. This means that he limits the soul to its rational part.[30] He denies the immortality of the soul, rejecting Plato's teaching on this point.[31] Everything that is born must also perish, and the soul has to be born, since a child resembles his parents not only physically but also mentally; moreover, the soul can feel pain and fall ill, hence it can also perish.[32]

Panaetius defines the moral end as living according to the impulses nature has given us,[33] and he adds, contrary to Zeno and Chrysippus, that virtue is not self-sufficient, but that we need health, strength, and wealth.[34] He distinguishes two kinds of virtue—one theoretical and the other practical.[35] Happiness, which is living in accordance with nature, is the common end of all virtues, but everyone reaches this end in a different way.[36] This means that for Panaetius virtue and happiness have an individualistic character, and this is an original and characteristic aspect of his moral outlook to which we

28. Van Straaten, fr. 74.

29. Cic., *Tusc.* 1.42; Van Straaten, fr. 83.

30. Van Straaten, fr. 85, 86 (from Tertullian and Nemesius).

31. Cic., *Tusc.* 1.79; Van Straaten, fr. 83.

32. Van Straaten, fr. 83.

33. Van Straaten, fr. 96 (from Clement of Alexandria).

34. Diog. Laert. 7.128; Van Straaten, fr. 110.

35. Diog. Laert. 7.92; Van Straaten, fr. 108.

36. Stobaeus, *Eclogae*, 2.7; Van Straaten, fr. 109.

shall return. He admits that pain is always bad and rejects the Stoic ideal of the complete absence of pain and of passion.[37] To a young man who asked him if the wise man could or should love, Panaetius answered: Let us leave aside the wise man, but as for you and me, who are far from being wise men, we should avoid love.[38]

We also know that Panaetius discussed with Polybius the merits of the Roman constitution and that he dealt in a concrete and practical way with politics, laws, and magistrates, as we learn from two passages in Cicero.[39] Some scholars have tried to trace back to Panaetius what Cicero says on the subject in the *De re publica* and the *De legibus,* and what Polybius says on the Roman republic and its institutions.

We are better informed about Panaetius' treatise on the duties (*De officiis*). According to the testimonies of Gellius and of Cicero himself, the three books by Panaetius on the duties are the principal source for the first two books by Cicero on the same subject.[40] Quoting the second book of Panaetius, Gellius affirms that the active man must guard against fortune's unexpected blows and the snares of the wicked.[41] Here we note the fight between virtue and fortune, a theme often recurrent in Plutarch and Polybius and in popular Stoicism. Cicero himself states in a letter that in the first two books of the *De officiis* he deals with what Panaetius had discussed in

37. Gellius, *Noctes Atticae* 12.5.10; Cic., *De fin.* 4.23; Van Straaten, fr. 111 and 113.

38. Seneca, *Epistolae* 116.5; Van Straaten, fr. 114.

39. Cic., *De re publica* 1.34; Cicero, *De legibus* 3.14; Van Straaten, fr. 119 and 48.8

40. Cic., *Ep. ad Atticum* 16.11; Gellius 13.28; Van Straaten, fr. 34 and 116.

41. Gellius 13.28.

his three books on the proper (*kathekon*). Cicero wants to deal with a problem omitted by Panaetius—namely, what is proper according to the circumstances—and on this theme, which he will then treat in his third book, he will use as his source a treatise by Posidonius. Cicero in the same letter says that he wants to translate the proper (*kathekon*) of Panaetius as duty (*De officiis*).[42] We have here one of the characteristic and well-documented cases of how a Greek philosophical term was translated by Cicero into Latin, then later retranslated into all the modern Western languages. We note as well how these translations in turn led to the transformation of the concept. For Panaetius, as also for Zeno, the proper (*kathekon*) indicates what should be done in various particular circumstances, and it is clearly stated that this is a relative good different from the perfect good of virtue.[43] Instead the Latin term *officium* indicates rather an absolute, not simply a relative obligation, and finally the German term of Kant (*Pflicht*) corresponds to a general obligation (as then applied to particular circumstances) and becomes almost identical with virtue itself.

Cicero notes at the beginning of his work that he will follow the Stoics and especially Panaetius, not as a simple translator but as an independent author who chooses from his source what he deems appropriate, following his own judgment.[44] He repeats several times that he is freely following the Stoic doctrine of Panaetius and adds that the Academic school to which he belongs permits him to take from other schools what seems to him probable.[45]

---

42. Cic., *Ep. ad Atticum* 16.11; Van Straaten, fr. 34. In his third book Cicero also uses Hecaton, another student of Panaetius (*De officiis* 3.63).

43. Cic., *De off.* 1.46.

44. Cic., *De off.* 1.6–7; Van Straaten, fr. 39.

45. Cic., *De off.* 2.60, 3.7, 3.20. See Van Straaten, fr. 122 and 35.

In the course of the two books the name of Panaetius is quoted often, and we have good reason to attribute to him the greater part of their contents. It seems that Panaetius did not give a definition of *kathekon*,[46] and that is not surprising since the term and the concept were well known since the time of Zeno. He distinguishes between general and practical duties, or perfect and common duties. The common duties are the theme of his treatise.[47] Panaetius states that there are three types of deliberation—that is, we must decide if something is good or evil; if it is useful or not; and whether we should follow the good or what seems useful when they appear to be in conflict.[48] Cicero adds that one can also deliberate on the degrees of the good and the useful, a point Panaetius apparently omitted.[49] According to traditional Stoic doctrine, all animals by nature try to preserve themselves, but man, being rational, extends his care from the present to the past and to the future.[50] Care of the family is a part of this tendency toward self-preservation.[51] We also have an innate tendency toward the knowledge of truth, toward freedom, as well as toward domination.[52] In addition, we have an innate appreciation for decorum and beauty, both with regard to visible things and to thoughts or to actions,[53] and we further have a form or idea of the moral good, as Plato saw it.[54]

46. Cic., *De off.* 1.7; Van Straaten, fr. 39.

47. Cic., *De off.* 1.7–8.

48. Cic., *De off.* 1.9; Van Straaten, fr. 99.

49. Cic., *De off.* 1.7; Van Straaten, fr. 39.

50. Cic., *De off.* 1.11; Van Straaten, fr. 98.

51. Cic., *De off.* 1.12; Van Straaten, fr. 98.

52. Cic., *De off.* 1.13; Van Straaten, fr. 98.

53. Cic., *De off.* 1.14; Van Straaten, fr. 98.

54. Cic., *De off.* 1.14: Formam quidem ipsam . . . et tamquam

The moral good (*kalon*) is rendered by Cicero as *honestum*, a translation that makes one think of honor and honesty and does not convey too well the original Greek concept, and this has been the cause of much subsequent confusion. The moral good, in turn, is based on the four cardinal virtues.[55]

After this introduction Cicero goes on to a series of rules regarding prudence, justice, fortitude, and temperance. In the long section on justice he also discusses benevolence and insists that the men among whom we live are not wise and possess at the most merely some image of virtue,[56] a passage that alludes again to Panaetius' view that the wise man in reality does not exist. Cicero then talks of the human race as a universal community and society that has as its bond reason and discourse (*ratio et oratio*, probably a double Latin translation of the single Greek word *logos*), a bond that unites all men in a natural society.[57] Animals are not part of this community, and so they do not participate in the ties of justice, equity, and goodness that unite all men.[58] According to the Stoics, animals do not have the rights believed in today, but the protection of animals depends on the obligations man has also toward them. We have here a theory upon which the concept of *humanitas* is based, a concept that is often considered typically Roman

---

faciem honesti vides, quae si oculis videretur, mirabiles amores, ut ait Plato, excitaret sapientiae (see Plato, *Symposium*, 211e—-212a).

55. Cic., *De off.* 1.14.

56. Cic., *De off.* 1.46: vivitur non cum perfectis hominibus planeque sapientibus, sed cum iis, in quibus praeclare agitur si sunt simulacra virtutis.

57. Cic., *De off.* 1.50.

58. Ibid.

rather than Greek. It is expressed in the famous saying of Terence (who was also a member of the circle of Scipio the Younger): "I am a man: I consider nothing human to be foreign to me."[59] And here we may also remember a famous passage of Gellius in which two meanings of the Latin concept of *humanitas* are discussed. One is defined as benevolence toward all men and corresponds to the Greek concept of *philanthropia* (which is hence the source of the Latin *humanitas*). The other meaning deals with education in the humane or liberal arts and corresponds to the Greek term *paideia*.[60] Gellius, who emphasizes the second meaning of *humanitas* and treats the first nearly with scorn, does indicate that also the first one is derived from the Greek. I am inclined to think that the Terentian and Ciceronian concept of *humanitas* reflects a concept of Panaetius. The ambiguity of the term and the confusion of the two meanings were used by the humanists to give a moralistic and humanitarian color to what was their cultural ideal. In the hands of our contemporaries it has served to substitute for the culture of humanism a brand of sentimental philanthropy that is about to deprive humanistic culture of its traditional place in the schools and universities and to take over the institutions and resources originally established for it.

Speaking of fortitude Cicero says that it cannot be separated from justice[61] and that its motivation should not be the thirst for fame.[62] He then quotes Panaetius for a dictum of Scipio that men corrupted by good fortune must be tamed like horses

---

59. Cic., *De off.* 1.30 (see Terence, *Heauton Timorumenos* 1:1.25: homo sum: humani nil a me alienum puto).

60. Gellius 13.17.1.

61. Cic., *De off.* 1.68.

62. Cic., *De off.* 1.65.

by reason and instruction so that they can understand the fragility of human affairs and the vicissitudes of fortune.[63]

Speaking on temperance, Cicero treats at length the concept of decorum (*prepon*). Following again Panaetius, he insists that decorum is inseparable from virtue in general and from each particular virtue.[64] General decorum is defined as what agrees with the excellence of man as distinguished from the other animals.[65] Here we have one of the roots of the doctrine of the dignity of man that enjoyed a special place in the thought of the fifteenth and sixteenth centuries, as it has in our own century in a different sense. In a more special sense, decorum is bound to the virtue of temperance.[66] The concept of decorum had its origins in the rhetorical and poetic traditions at least since Aristotle. It seems that it was Panaetius who transferred it into the field of ethics, thus giving an aesthetic aspect to his moral doctrine. Every man has two "personae," one in common with all men and the other particular to each individual.[67] Therefore every man must preserve the decorum common to all men as well as his own proper decorum. There are differences in character between various persons that do not always indicate a different degree of morality.[68] We can observe in this an individualistic element in the ethics of Panaetius that is absent from orthodox Stoic doctrine. Just as the actor can choose the part he wants to play in the theater, so the moral man can choose the part he wants to play in the

63. Cic., *De off.* 1.90; Van Straaten, fr. 12.
64. Cic., *De off.* 1.93–95; Van Straaten, fr. 170.
65. Cic., *De off.* 1.96; Van Straaten, fr. 107.
66. Cic., *De off.* 1.107.
67. Ibid.
68. Cic., *De off.* 1.109–10; Van Straaten, fr. 97.

theater of life.[69] Also, the metaphor of life as a theater has a long history, and it probably does not begin with Panaetius (there are even some traces in Plato), but, especially through Cicero, he did have a significant role in it.

The choice between various goods, mentioned by Cicero at the end of the first book, was not taken from Panaetius,[70] but Cicero returns to following Panaetius in the second book when he speaks of the useful. As the Latin *honestum* corresponds to the *kalon* of the Stoics, I believe that the useful corresponds to the *agathon*.[71] Listing useful things, Cicero and Panaetius follow not only the true but also the probable.[72] We learn that Panaetius did not compare between the various useful things or between the good and the useful,[73] but he accepts with Zeno that the moral good is useful.[74]

The third book of the *De officiis* contains a long and important passage that explains the meaning of the entire work and that seems to reflect closely Panaetius' own concept. The true moral good (*honestum*) is found only in the perfect sages. Those who are not perfect sages do not possess the perfect good but only a copy of it. The *officia* spoken of in these books are called intermediary (*media*) by the Stoics; they are found everywhere and can be obtained with the aid of ingenuity and doctrine. Instead the *officium* called true (*rectum*), perfect, and absolute is only found in the wise man. Common people accept as perfect what is not, as they do in their judgments on poetry

69. Cic., *De off.* 1.114.

70. Cic., *De off.* 1.152, 161; see Van Straaten, fr. 36.

71. Cic., *De off.* 2.10.

72. Cic., *De off.* 2.51; Van Straaten, fr. 95.

73. Cic., *De off.* 3.7–11; Van Straaten, fr. 35.

74. Cic., *De off.* 3.12; Van Straaten, fr. 101.

and paintings. The *officia* we are discussing are goods of a secondary level and are found in men of any type and not only in the sages; even famous men who are called sages in common usage are not wise men in the perfect sense of the philosophers, but only have a semblance of wisdom.[75]

The concept of moral decorum that is characteristic of Panaetius has led various scholars to suspect his influence also in Philodemus and in the *ars poetica* of Horace, as well as in certain passages of Cicero's *Orator*. I should also add an old hypothesis of mine that the introduction to the *Orator*, a famous and much discussed passage in which Cicero tries to describe the perfect orator, also reflects at least partially the influence of Panaetius:

> Consequently in delineating the perfect orator I shall be portraying such a one as perhaps has never existed. Indeed I am not inquiring who was the perfect orator, but what is that unsurpassable ideal. . . . But I am firmly of the opinion that nothing of any kind is so beautiful as not to be excelled in beauty by that of which it is a copy, as a mask is a copy of a face. This ideal cannot be perceived by the eye or ear, nor by any of the senses, but we can nevertheless grasp it by the mind and the imagination. For example, in the case of the statues of Phidias, the most perfect of their kind that we have ever seen, and in the case of the paintings I have mentioned, we can, in spite of their beauty, imagine something more beautiful. Surely that great sculptor, while making the image of Jupiter or Minerva, did not look at any person whom he was using as a model, but in his own mind there dwelt a surpassing vision [*species*] of beauty; at this he gazed and intent on this he guided his artist's hand to produce the

75. Cic., *De off.* 3.14–18.

likeness of the god. Accordingly, as there is something perfect and surpassing in the case of sculpture and painting—an intellectual ideal by reference to which the artist represents those objects which do not themselves appear to the eye—so with our minds we conceive the ideal of perfect eloquence, but with our ears we catch only the copy. These patterns of things are called ἰδέαι or ideas by Plato, that eminent master and teacher both of style and thought; these, he says, do not "become"; they exist forever, and depend on intellect and reason; other things come into being and cease to be, they are in flux and do not remain long in the same state. Whatever, then, is to be discussed rationally and methodically, must be reduced to the ultimate form and type of its class.[76]

This concept of the idea of the perfect orator is taken up again in various other passages of Cicero's *Orator*,[77] and these passages have many elements in common with the ideas of Panaetius as reported in the *De officiis* and elsewhere. They speak of decorum and of the analogy between the arts and life.[78] We should also remember the passages in which Panaetius indicates that the Stoic sage does not exist but is simply an ideal concept that should be imitated by those who are not wise men, but who are trying to approach wisdom.[79]

I am hence inclined to attribute to Panaetius the interpretation of the Platonic idea that we find at the beginning of the

76. Cicero, *Orator* 7–10, trans. H. M. Hubbell, in *Cicero*, vol. 5, Loeb Classics (Cambridge: Harvard University Press, 1971), pp. 311–13. All subsequent references are to this edition. In this case, we did not attempt to give a new translation of the Latin text.

77. Cic., *Orator* 18, 19, 101.

78. Cic., *Orator* 36, 70–71, 74.

79. Cic., *De off.* 3.13–17, 1.14. Sen., *Epist.* 116.

Orator. It seems probable to me that Panaetius made an analogous discourse with regard to the sage, and that Cicero in his rhetorical work transferred the concept from the sage to the perfect orator, that is, from the art of living to the art of rhetoric. The difference between the concept of the idea as we find it in the writings of Plato and as it is interpreted here is notable, but also interesting and historically significant. The idea that for Plato has its own transcendent reality independent of the thought that grasps it was reduced by Antisthenes and by the Stoics to a simple concept (*ennoia*) in our mind. Panaetius, as we know from various testimonies and other examples, admired Plato and had the tendency to give to the Stoic doctrine a more Platonic coloring. Treating the Platonic idea as an ideal or normative concept in our mind, Panaetius accepted the reduction by the Cynics and Stoics of the Platonic idea to a simple concept, but he added to it a valid and normative element that it had lacked until then. We are on the road that will lead to the idea as concept and thought in the mind of God, a doctrine of which we shall speak again subsequently.

As the analogy between ethics as the *ars vitae* and the other arts is a concept common to the Stoics, it also seems probable to me that Panaetius developed the analogy between the ideal wise man and the perfect sculpture and painting, while the application to rhetoric and to the perfect orator is probably an addition by Cicero who, despite his philosophical preparation, thought of himself more than anything else as an orator and as a theorist of rhetoric.

There is still another notable and interesting difference between the Platonic idea and its rendering in Panaetius and Cicero. The idea of Plato is a general and abstract concept, like the good, the beautiful, and the just, and the particular attribute that corresponds to the general concept belongs only to the concrete object inasmuch as it participates in the idea. Hence, for Plato, a particular beautiful thing, even if most perfect, is not an idea but a particular object that participates in the idea to a relatively perfect degree. This distinction between the idea and the most perfect particular, which is obvious in Plato (for whom, e.g., the perfect republic is not an idea but a particular object of thought that participates perfectly in the idea of the just) disappears in Panaetius and Cicero when the Platonic idea loses its absolute existence and becomes a simple concept of our thought. This concept was again taken up by many later thinkers through Kant (who also puts the ideas in the human mind), and the concept of the ideal as abstract noun (which appears only in the eighteenth century and was probably coined by Diderot) presupposes the transformation of the Platonic idea due to Antisthenes and Zeno and then to Panaetius and Cicero.

The importance of Panaetius in the history of ancient thought is not always appreciated or recognized as it should be. His moderation vis-à-vis Zeno and Chrysippus, and his concern for the moral duties of the ordinary person rather than of the wise man, brought him closer to the daily life and the politics of his time, both in Greece and in Rome, where it exercised a notable influence. He modified the Stoic doctrine of the accord of the moral man with nature, insisting on the dignity of man in general and on the characteristic, but morally neutral, differences between single persons. He transferred the concept of decorum from rhetoric and poetics to moral philosophy and so gave to ethics as an art of living a new aesthetic coloring. It also seems he formulated a concept of *humanitas* that included both moral and cultural elements, and we suspect some traces of his influence in Terence who was close to the circle of Scipio the Younger. Interpreting the Platonic idea as a moral and artistic concept present in our mind and as the ideal model for every imitation, he had a lasting influence in the history of the interpretation (often false) of the Platonic Idea, and he appears as well as a late representative of that classical Greek spirit that does not forget and does not enjoy the evils of this life, but tries to overcome them with clarity of thought and serenity of spirit. In this sense he was a worthy successor, not only of Zeno and Chrysippus but also of Homer and Sophocles, of Plato and Epicurus.

CHAPTER SEVEN

Posidonius

Posidonius of Apamea, the great disciple of Panaetius, was at least the equal of his teacher in importance and influence, but his philosophical position was much different. The reconstruction of his thought offers the same and perhaps even greater difficulties. We have a certain number of direct quotations, but many doctrines have been attributed to him simply because they are found in books by Cicero for which Posidonius is considered the main source, though he is not explicitly quoted in the relevant passages. The reconstruction proposed by Karl Reinhardt is very suggestive and for the most part quite convincing, but it can be accepted as definitive only when it is based on explicit quotations from Posidonius. A collection of fragments and pertinent testimonies did not exist until relatively recent times. Now we have two, of which one, edited by Theiler, includes all the anonymous passages in Cicero attributed to Posidonius by modern scholars, while the other one, edited by Edelstein and Kidd, is limited to the sources where Posidonius is mentioned explicitly. I prefer to base my rather summary interpretation on the edition of Edelstein and Kidd, and to treat the additional attributions of Reinhardt and Theiler, with due respect, as hypothetical.

Posidonius was born circa 135 B.C. and was the student of Panaetius in Athens. He made long voyages and opened a school at Rhodes where he had many students and was also visited by important personages like Cicero and Pompey; he died around 51 B.C. His fame and influence lasted for several centuries. Unlike Panaetius, moral philosophy does not occupy the center of his thought; he was rather a scientist and a scholar of truly encyclopedic interests. On the other hand, he returned to Stoic orthodoxy on many points where Panaetius had abandoned it. Like Panaetius, Posidonius too had a profound interest in the work of Plato and of Aristotle, but the nature of his interest was quite different from that of Panaetius, as we shall see.

Posidonius was famous in his time as the most learned of the philosophers,[1] and the traces of his work are found in many areas of knowledge. He distinguished himself in the field of historiography and wrote a continuation of the history of Polybius, a rather long work from which many fragments have been preserved.[2] In them he shows great interest for

1. Posidonius, *The Fragments,* ed. L. Edelstein and I. G. Kidd, vol. 1, *Testimonia* (henceforth, T) 48; and *Poseidonios: Die Fragmente,* ed. W. Theiler, vol. 1, *Testimonia* (henceforth, T) 2c.

2. Edelstein-Kidd, fr. 51–78; Theiler, fr. 80–250.

historical particulars, for the customs of various peoples and for anthropology; the lively and rhetorical style of this work was much praised by ancient critics.[3] We also have many passages by Posidonius dealing with geography and found in the same historical work.[4]

Through Seneca we know the theory of Posidonius on the origin of civilization.[5] He has human history begin with a golden age that was governed by the philosophers. He attributes to the philosophers and sages the invention of all arts and crafts, including agriculture, weaving, and pottery, and considers Democritus to be the inventor of the architectural arch.

We know a good deal about Posidonius the geographer since he is frequently quoted as a source by Strabo, especially for the local customs and the physical and meteorological conditions of many parts of the Mediterranean world. Thus we learn that Posidonius traveled in Spain, spent thirty days at Gades (Cadiz) where he made scientific observations, and stopped in Gaul and Italy on his return to Greece.[6] Strabo quotes him on the rivers and volcanoes of various regions, for the distances between different places, and for other information of the kind. He did not limit himself to describing the observed facts as such, but always sought to give them scientific explanations since his interest in geography was clearly linked to his interests and studies in meteorology, astronomy, and mathematics. Quoting his writing on the Ocean, Strabo adds that it contained many elements of geography and math-

3. Edelstein-Kidd, T 103; Theiler, fr. 19.

4. Theiler, fr. 19.

5. Edelstein-Kidd, fr. 286; Theiler, fr. 448 (Seneca, *Epistolae* 90).

6. Edelstein-Kidd, fr. 19, 49, 218, 269, 274; Theiler, fr. 274, 13, 26, 25, 34.

ematics.[7] Strabo observes that Posidonius offered many causal explanations and in this respect was like Aristotle rather than the other Stoics who consider the causes as obscure.[8] We know explicitly, again from Strabo, that Posidonius treated geography in a physical and mathematical context.[9] Also Galen says that Posidonius, different from the other Stoics, was well prepared in geometry and accustomed to offering precise demonstrations.[10]

We learn from many sources of the particular contributions made by Posidonius to the various sciences, such as physical geography, meteorology, astronomy, and mathematics. Especially famous was his study of the Ocean and of the tides based on the observations he had made at Gades. Posidonius basically says that the movement of the sea is periodical according to day, month, and year, and that it has a certain affinity with the movement of the moon.[11] This theory is substantially correct, but one must be aware of a characteristic concept used by Posidonius here and elsewhere which has been rightly underscored by Reinhardt: the movement of the sea follows the movement of the moon according to an intrinsic and universal principle of affinity (*sumpatheia*) that unites the various parts of the world with each other and gives them not only spatial coexistence but also a vital and dynamic unity as well.[12]

7. Edelstein-Kidd, fr. 49; Theiler, fr. 13.

8. Edelstein-Kidd, T 85; Theiler, T 30b.

9. Edelstein-Kidd, T 77; Theiler, T 31.

10. Edelstein-Kidd, T 83; Theiler, fr. 408.

11. Edelstein-Kidd, fr. 217, lines 30ff. (Strabo, *Geographia* 3.5.8); Theiler, fr. 26.

12. Edelstein-Kidd, fr. 106, line 17 (Cicero, *De divinatione* 2.34); Theiler, fr. 379.

As for physical geography, Posidonius modified the traditional theory of five zones, increasing their number with subdivisions and considering the hot zone to be inhabited.[13] He attempted to calculate with precision the size of the earth[14] and also that of the sun.[15] He tried to explain the eclipse of the sun,[16] and he offered a theory of the winds, quoting Aristotle.[17] He even built a model of the spherical universe that explained the movements of the various stars[18] and tried to determine the size and substance of the moon and to explain the Milky Way, the rainbow, lightning, hail, and the comets. In his explanation of the aura he followed Aristotle.[19]

Also notable was Posidonius' contribution to geometry, as we learn particularly from the commentary of Proclus on Euclid. He offered new definitions of the problem, the theorem, and of parallel lines.[20] He identifies the geometric figure with the line that encloses it rather than with the enclosed space,[21] and he offers a definition of quadrangles.[22] He wrote a whole book in defense of geometry against the Epicurean Zeno of Sidon who had attacked it.[23] Among the arguments he uses we find one of great methodological interest: "Epicurus himself, as also the other philosophers do, admits that many

13. Edelstein-Kidd, fr. 210; Theiler, fr. 283.

14. Edelstein-Kidd, fr. 49, 202; Theiler, fr. 13, 287.

15. Edelstein-Kidd, fr. 19, 114–115; Theiler, fr. 274, 290a.

16. Edelstein-Kidd, fr. 123; Theiler, fr. 291.

17. Edelstein-Kidd, fr. 137a; Theiler, fr. 5.

18. Edelstein-Kidd, T 86; Theiler, fr. 361 (p. 277).

19. Edelstein-Kidd, fr. 122, 130, 134, 135, 136, 132, 133; Theiler, fr. 301, 298a, 323, 325, 318, 322, 315.

20. Edelstein-Kidd, fr. 195, 197; Theiler, fr. 464, 467.

21. Edelstein-Kidd, fr. 196; Theiler, fr. 465.

22. Edelstein-Kidd, fr. 198; Theiler, fr. 466.

23. Edelstein-Kidd, fr. 46; Theiler, fr. 463.

things that are simply possible and even many things impossible are often assumed by reason of their consequences."[24] I do not think that this is a casual remark, but I see in it the trace of an authentic theory of the hypothesis that permits us to assume, on the basis of their verified consequences, things unproved or unprovable in themselves.

This theory of the hypothesis is attested with more details in a long passage from the compendium by Geminus of the meteorology of Posidonius, which is quoted by Simplicius word for word.[25] The passage takes its start from Aristotle and tries to define the borders between physics and astronomy, two distinct but closely linked subjects of study whose relationship presented serious difficulties for Aristotle himself and continued to present them for all the thinkers of the Middle Ages and of the Renaissance until Galileo. According to Posidonius, the theory of physics considers the substance of the heaven and of the stars and their force, quality, generation, and corruption and can offer demonstrations regarding their size, shape, and order. Astronomy, on the other hand, does not treat of these things but of the order of the heavenly bodies. It shows that the sky is truly an order (*kosmos*) and deals with the shapes, sizes, and distances of the earth, the moon, and the sun; the eclipses and the conjunctions of the stars; and the quantity and quality of their movements. When it deals with quantity and quality, astronomy needs arithmetic and geometry. The physicist and the astronomer often deal with the same subject—like the size of the sun or the shape of the earth—but they do not proceed in the same way. One (the physicist) demonstrates everything starting from substance or

24. Edelstein-Kidd, fr. 47, lines 72–75; Theiler, fr. 463.
25. Edelstein-Kidd, fr. 18; Theiler, fr. 255.

from the fact that it is better this way or from generation and transformation. The other (the astronomer) starts from the accidents of the shapes and sizes or from the quantity of movement and from the time corresponding to it. The physicist looks to active force and touches often on cause; instead the astronomer, when he bases his proofs on external accidents, is not a sufficient viewer of the cause . . . and sometimes does not even desire to grasp the cause . . . and sometimes finds by hypothesis some modalities whose existence will maintain the phenomena intact. Of this type are the eccentric circles or the epicycles introduced to explain the movements of the planets. We must go over all the modalities by which these phenomena can be produced so that the theory of planets corresponds to a causal explanation (*aitiologia*) after a possible fashion. Mentioning the heliocentric system of Heraclides of Pontus, Posidonius states that it is not for the astronomer to know what is immobile by its nature and what are the immobile things; rather he introduces some hypotheses on things mobile and immobile and looks for the hypotheses to which the celestial phenomena correspond. But the astronomer must take certain fundamental principles from the physicist, namely that the movements of the stars are simple and uniform. This passage, coming from the greatest philosopher of Antiquity (after Aristotle) who was also a great scientist, is of extraordinary importance. It not only distinguishes between physics and astronomy as separate sciences but says that astronomy does not delve into the substance and quality of the heavenly bodies, and is content to propose hypotheses whose truth it does not seek to prove but which serve to explain actually observed celestial phenomena. The motto *sozein ta phainomena*, emphasized by historians of the natural sciences for various epochs of Western thought, was clearly formulated by Posidonius—indeed, he seems to have been the first to use it.[26] Astronomy is thus established as an empirical and pragmatic science based on observation and detached from physics, which remains a demonstrative and deductive science according to the Aristotelian tradition.

Posidonius, like the majority of the Hellenistic philosophers, accepts the threefold division of philosophy into logic, physics, and ethics—a division invented, or at least formalized, by Xenocrates. But like Panaetius he begins with physics, and he seems to have dealt very little with logic. He insists that the three parts are not separate one from the other but are closely bound together and inseparable. Philosophy is compared to an animal whose flesh and blood are physics, whose bones and nerves are logic, and whose soul represents ethics.[27] We can observe here, as Reinhardt points out, the organic tendency that is characteristic of all of Posidonius' thought and is manifest in many particular points of his doctrine.

In Posidonius' case we can even speak of a primacy of physics,[28] which leads him to subordinate all the other arts and sciences to philosophy. This tendency is implicit in what he says on physics and astronomy and in the concept of the philosopher as the inventor of all the arts and sciences, points we have already mentioned. It reappears in a classification of the arts preserved by Seneca.[29] There are four different groups of arts: the vulgar arts are those of the craftsmen; the pleasant arts (*ludicrae*) are those that entertain the public; third are the

26. P. Duhem, *Sozein ta phainomena, Essai sur la notion de théorie physique de Platon à Galilée*, reprinted from *Annales de Philosophie Chrétienne* no. 155, ser. 4, no. 6 (1908): 9–11.

27. Edelstein-Kidd, fr. 88; Theiler, fr. 252b.

28. Edelstein-Kidd, fr. 91; Theiler, fr. 253.

29. Edelstein-Kidd, fr. 90 (Sen., *Epist.* 88.21–28); Theiler, fr. 447.

arts called puerile—that is, the encyclopedic arts often called the liberal arts; and finally there are the true liberal arts, which train for virtue and wisdom and which in this sense belong to philosophy.

Of the physics of Posidonius we have preserved some definitions of fundamental concepts, such as matter, generation, and corruption or cause.[30] We also have a definition of God: he is an intellectual and fiery spirit (*pneuma*), he has no shape, but transforms himself into everything he wants to be, and thus he resembles everything.[31] As a good Stoic, Posidonius places fate together with God and nature[32] and accepts the periodic destruction of the universe.[33] The space outside the world is not infinite, but only sufficient to make the destruction of the world possible.[34] Posidonius treats heaven as the governing part of the world,[35] and the world as an animal and as the substance—that is, the matter—of God.[36] He accepts the determinism of the first Stoics and their theory of divination that depends on it.[37] On this point he is often quoted and used by Cicero. Posidonius distinguishes two forms of divination, natural and artificial, and insists on the prescience of dying people.[38] According to Cicero, Posidonius also distinguished three different forms of dreams. In one type of dream, the soul itself foresees the future because it has an affinity

30. Edelstein-Kidd, fr. 92, 96, 95; Theiler, fr. 267, 268, 269.
31. Edelstein-Kidd, fr. 101; Theiler, fr. 349.
32. Edelstein-Kidd, fr. 103; Theiler, fr. 382a.
33. Edelstein-Kidd, fr. 97; Theiler, fr. 302.
34. Edelstein-Kidd, fr. 97; Theiler, fr. 302.
35. Edelstein-Kidd, fr. 23; Theiler, fr. 347.
36. Edelstein-Kidd, fr. 13, 20; Theiler, fr. 304, 344.
37. Edelstein-Kidd, fr. 25, 27; Theiler, fr. 381, 371a.
38. Edelstein-Kidd, fr. 26, 108; Theiler, fr. 371b, 372, 373a.

with the gods; in a second type, the air is full of immortal souls upon which the marks of the truth are imprinted; in a third type, the gods themselves speak to those asleep. Therefore, all the capacity for divination, according to Posidonius, is derived from God, from fate, and from nature.[39] He believes that nature itself contains signs of the future.[40] Posidonius wrote no less than five books on divination,[41] and Cicero quotes him and criticizes him repeatedly in his work *De divinatione*,[42] and also quotes him in the *De fato*.[43]

We have a certain number of interesting testimonies on Posidonius' conception of the soul. He calls vision a sort of growing together (*sumphusis*), namely between the eye and its object.[44] He says there is a psychic spirit (*pneuma*) even within the bones of the animals.[45] Criticizing the Epicureans, Posidonius states that it is not the bodies that hold together (*sunekhei*) the souls, but the souls that hold together the bodies like glue joins itself and the external things.[46]

Several passages indicate a tendency of Posidonius to lessen the complete separation between the soul and the body. There are psychic things and corporeal things, but also corporeal things that are not psychic but which concern the soul, and on the other hand psychic things that are not corporeal but concern the body. Things simply psychic are those that happen in

39. Edelstein-Kidd, fr. 107, 108; Theiler, fr. 377, 373a. See Cic., *De div.* 1.64 and 125.

40. Edelstein-Kidd, fr. 110; Theiler, fr. 378.

41. Edelstein-Kidd, fr. 26; Theiler, fr. 371b.

42. Edelstein-Kidd, fr. 106, 109; Theiler, fr. 379, 380a.

43. Edelstein-Kidd, fr. 104; Theiler, fr. 386.

44. Edelstein-Kidd, fr. 194b; Theiler, fr. 395c.

45. Edelstein-Kidd, fr. 28b; Theiler, fr. 389b.

46. Edelstein-Kidd, fr. 149; Theiler, fr. 400a.

decisions or opinions, like desires, fears, or angers. Things simply corporeal are fevers, shudders, pulse beat, and lung porosity. Things corporeal but concerning the soul are lethargies, melancholies, flights of phantasy, or depressions. Things psychic that concern the body are tremors, pallor, and changes of sensation due to fear or pain.[47]

We have several reports that indicate that Posidonius tried to interpret certain passages of the *Timaeus* and of other works by Plato, but it is by no means sure that he composed an actual commentary on the *Timaeus,* as one sometimes reads. In Plutarch we read that Posidonius, referring to a passage of the *Timaeus,* defined the soul as a form or idea of what is extended in the universe, according to a number that comprehends a composite harmony. He goes on to state that mathematical beings occupy an intermediate place between intelligible and sensible things, and that also the soul has an intermediate position between intelligible and sensible things, since it is eternal like intelligible things but has a passive part (*pathetikon*) like corporeal things.[48] Evidently the word "idea" in this passage does not indicate the Platonic idea, but simply a form. This also explains a passage in Macrobius, which simply says that Posidonius defined the soul as an idea.[49] Evidently, Macrobius is giving a partial summary of the passage (of which we have an ampler quotation in Plutarch), and there is no need to attribute to Posidonius the opinion that the soul is a Platonic idea.

We have other testimonies that Posidonius studied and interpreted the text of certain passages in the *Timaeus.* Explaining the *Timaeus* of Plato, Posidonius states (as Sextus Empiri-

47. Edelstein-Kidd, fr. 154; Theiler, fr. 436.
48. Edelstein-Kidd, fr. 141a; Theiler, fr. 391a.
49. Edelstein-Kidd, fr. 140; Theiler, fr. 391b.

cus says) that light is perceived by vision, which is suited to light, and that voice is perceived by hearing that is like the air, so by analogy the nature of all things must be perceived by reason (*logos*), which is suited to it.[50] According to Theon of Smyrna, Posidonius also offers an explanation of another passage in the *Timaeus* in which Plato has the soul composed of seven numbers. According to Posidonius, day and night have the nature of even and odd, and the month is composed of four weeks.[51] I think that the odd corresponds to the number one and the even to the number two. Posidonius also quoted the *Timaeus* about Atlantis.[52] All of these explanations of passages in the *Timaeus* demonstrate that Posidonius studied this dialogue of Plato with great care, but they are not sufficient to attribute to Posidonius a commentary on the *Timaeus*. Posidonius quotes and explains other works of Plato as well: a propos of the famous passage in the *Phaedrus* on the origin of the soul, we learn that according to Posidonius this is only applicable to the world soul.[53] According to a passage in Seneca, Posidonius criticized Plato for having premised his laws with introductions since laws, to be effective, must be brief.[54] As we shall see later, Posidonius was also influenced by Plato in his theory of the parts of the soul.

Little is known of the logic of Posidonius. We know he wrote a treatise on the criterion,[55] and we know a definition of his on dialectics: dialectics is the knowledge of things true and

50. Edelstein-Kidd, fr. 85; Theiler, fr. 395a, 461.

51. Edelstein-Kidd, fr. 291; Theiler, fr. 392.

52. Edelstein-Kidd, fr. 49, 297–300; Theiler, fr. 13 (Strabo, *Geographia* 2.3.6).

53. Edelstein-Kidd, fr. 290; Theiler, fr. 393.

54. Edelstein-Kidd, fr. 178; Theiler, fr. 451.

55. Edelstein-Kidd, fr. 42; Theiler, fr. 460.

false and of things neither true nor false.[56] What things neither true nor false are is not explained, but we may conjecture that they are probable things. It is interesting to note that Posidonius too wrote *Protreptikoi*—that is, an exhortation to the study of philosophy—and he claims that one should not abstain from philosophy because of the discrepancy (*diaphonia*) among the opinions of the various philosophers.[57] We should note that this discrepancy among the opinions of the philosophers was used by the Skeptics to refute all dogmatic philosophies. In a certain sense, the reflections of Posidonius we discussed earlier on the hypothesis and on methods of physics and astronomy ought to be considered as important contributions to logic as well.

We are much better informed on the ethics of Posidonius. On the basis of numerous testimonies one can conclude that Posidonius divorced himself from Stoic orthodoxy to a lesser degree than Panaetius. Diogenes Laertius cites him many times for having repeated and approved certain traditional Stoic doctrines, and Seneca reports that Posidonius defended explicitly and with a new argument of his own the dictum of Zeno that the sage is never drunk.[58] Cicero recounts that in his famous encounter with Pompey Posidonius insisted that only the moral good is good and that pain, harmful as it is, is not bad.[59] Unlike Panaetius, Posidonius holds that virtue is real, that the sage really does exist (and he cites as examples Socrates, Diogenes, and Antisthenes, who made great strides toward virtue).[60] He also spoke on nobility[61] and may have written a

---

56. Edelstein-Kidd, fr. 188; Theiler, fr. 454.
57. Edelstein-Kidd, fr. 1; Theiler, fr. 435c.
58. Edelstein-Kidd, fr. 175; Theiler, fr. 445a (Sen., *Epist.* 83.9–11).
59. Edelstein-Kidd, T 38; Theiler T 18.
60. Edelstein-Kidd, fr. 29; Theiler, fr. 403.
61. Edelstein-Kidd, T 12; Theiler doubts this.

specific treatise on the subject. It is probable that he defended there the Stoic doctrine that only the sage is noble. Of interest is his definition of man's end, which sounds more Aristotelian than Stoic. The end consists in a life that contemplates (*theo-rounta*) the truth and the order of all things and that prepares us as much as possible (to the accord with this order), without being moved by the irrational part of the soul.[62] We may note here the accent on contemplation and on the two parts of the soul, rational and irrational.

Posidonius developed also a new theory of the passions, and he criticized the doctrine of Chrysippus on that point, approaching the position of Plato and Aristotle. We are well informed on this part of the ethics of Posidonius by Galen, who quotes many passages word for word from the writings of Posidonius. According to Galen, Posidonius rejected the concept of distortion introduced by Chrysippus to explain the passions. He did not believe that vice came from the outside, but that its seed is in ourselves.[63] Whereas Zeno and Chrysippus had explained the passions as judgments and their consequences, Posidonius denies this theoretical origin for the passions and derives them instead from the irrational parts of the soul, which he calls (with Plato) the irascible part and the concupiscent part.[64] Hence, he admits an irrational element in the soul that is the cause of our passions,[65] and assigns to education the task of habituating the irrational and passive part of the soul to the government of the rational part.[66] Posidonius criticizes Chrysippus specifically on this point,

62. Edelstein-Kidd, fr. 186; Theiler, fr. 428.
63. Edelstein-Kidd, fr. 35; Theiler, fr. 423.
64. Edelstein-Kidd, fr. 34; Theiler, fr. 407.
65. Edelstein-Kidd, fr. 157; Theiler, fr. 407, 411.
66. Edelstein-Kidd, fr. 148; Theiler, fr. 406.

saying that passion cannot have its origins in reason and that another irrational faculty must be the cause through which the appetite exceeds the limits of reason.[67] According to Posidonius, Chrysippus contradicts both many evident phenomena and himself.[68] Denying, against Chrysippus, that emotions are based on opinions, Posidonius brought his own doctrine and that of Zeno himself closer to the Platonists.[69] He pays tribute to Plato, calling him divine, and approves in particular his doctrine of the passions and the faculties of the soul and adds that also the theories of the virtues and of the moral end—indeed, all the doctrines of moral philosophy—hang as from a thread on the Platonic doctrine of the faculties of the soul.[70]

We know in particular the criticism that Posidonius aimed at the definition, proposed by Chrysippus, of pain as recent opinion of the presence of an evil. He notes that pain often diminishes with time, even when the opinion of its presence remains the same.[71] We also have from nature, together with the other animals, a desire for pleasure and for power.[72] Posidonius speaks of a battle between reason and passion, and cites as authorities not only Plato and Aristotle but also Pythagoras.[73] The passions correspond to the movements of the passive and irrational part of the soul,[74] and these movements correspond to the disposition of our body, which in part comes from the mixture of the air in our "environment" (*periekhon*).[75]

67. Edelstein-Kidd, fr. 34; Theiler, fr. 407.

68. Edelstein-Kidd, T 83 and 99; Theiler, fr. 408.

69. Edelstein-Kidd, T 99; Theiler, fr. 408.

70. Edelstein-Kidd, fr. 150a (see fr. 30); Theiler, fr. 410 (see fr. 405).

71. Edelstein-Kidd, fr. 165; Theiler, fr. 410.

72. Edelstein-Kidd, fr. 158; Theiler, fr. 410.

73. Edelstein-Kidd, fr. 165, see T 95; Theiler, fr. 410.

74. Edelstein-Kidd, fr. 152; Theiler, fr. 411.

75. Edelstein-Kidd, fr. 169, 90–93; Theiler, fr. 416.

He is referring here to the well-known doctrine that has the character of men depend on the climate of the region they live in. The correspondence between the movements of the body and of the irrational part of the soul serves also to justify the doctrines of physiognomy, which presuppose an analogy between our body and our soul.[76]

The cause of the passions, that is, of disharmony and unhappy life, is due to the fact that we do not always follow the demon in us (which is related to and has the same nature as the demon that governs the entire universe), but that we sometimes follow a worse demon, the animal demon.[77] The principal condition for our happiness is that we are not swayed in any way by the irrational, unhappy, and atheistic part of our soul.[78] The command that we must live in accordance with nature means that we must follow the superior part of our soul.[79] Reason does not produce emotions except through the imagination. Emotions lessen with time, as we have seen in the case of pain, when the irrational part of the soul tires, and then reason has occasion to come forward. Posidonius uses also the analogy of the horse and the rider that derives from the *Phaedrus* of Plato.[80] Galen emphasizes and perhaps exaggerates Posidonius' agreement with Plato and Aristotle and his disagreement with Chrysippus. According to Galen, Aristotle and Posidonius do not speak of forms or parts of the soul but rather of faculties of the soul, which is of a single substance and has its seat in the heart.[81] We do not know how

76. Edelstein-Kidd, fr. 169, 84–85; Theiler, fr. 416.
77. Edelstein-Kidd, fr. 187, 4–9; Theiler, fr. 417.
78. Edelstein-Kidd, fr. 187, 11–13; Theiler, fr. 417.
79. Edelstein-Kidd, fr. 187, 16–21; Theiler, fr. 417.
80. Edelstein-Kidd, fr. 166; Theiler, fr. 417.
81. Edelstein-Kidd, fr. 146; Theiler, fr. 399.

Posidonius applied this theory to the definition of the virtues and to the other important parts of his moral philosophy.

The significance and the influence of Posidonius were notable, even if we do not consider the many important doctrines that have been attributed (with not very sound arguments) to him. He too was an eclectic, though of a very different kind from his teacher Panaetius. He abandoned the doctrine of Chrysippus, especially on the theory of the passions, and he moved closer to the position of Plato and Aristotle. He was a thinker and philosopher of notable stature and originality, but also a scholar and scientist of encyclopedic interests who made contributions to many fields of learning. I am inclined to believe with Reinhardt that Posidonius developed an organic and dynamic cosmology different from that of his predecessors and in which the concept of the world soul and of the affinity among the various parts of the universe played an important role. This concept recurs in Plotinus and in many Platonist or platonizing thinkers of the fifteenth and sixteenth centuries. But the opinion that the doctrine of the universe governed by a living soul and by the affinity (*sumpatheia*) of its parts stems from Posidonius remains uncertain, if plausible, since the concept and the term are attested to in Posidonius' name only twice—by Strabo on the tides and by Cicero in his discussion of divination. While the other thinkers we have spoken of or shall speak of contributed primarily to ethics and sometimes to logic and the theory of knowledge, Posidonius is clearly the Hellenistic thinker of the greatest merits in the various sectors of science and natural philosophy.

CHAPTER EIGHT

Antiochus of Ascalon

Having followed the fortunes of the Stoic school down to Panaetius and Posidonius, our final task is to describe the return of the Academy—after an interval of extreme and moderate Skepticism of about two hundred years—to a dogmatic position. This return was begun by Philo of Larissa, whom we have already discussed, and completed by Antiochus of Ascalon, of whom we must speak now. The change in position was announced as a return to the Old Academy of Plato and of his immediate successors, but in reality it led to an eclecticism that in Philo's case included many Platonic, Aristotelian, and Peripatetic doctrines, and in the case of Antiochus many typically Stoic elements as well.

Antiochus of Ascalon, whose birth date we do not know, was the student of Philo of Larissa as well as of the Stoic Mnesarchus. He became head of the Athenian Academy after the death of Philo about the year 88 B.C. and died around 68. He was in Rome in 88 B.C., and he accompanied Lucullus to Alexandria in 86 and again to the Orient in 69; he was one of the teachers of Cicero (who heard him talk in Athens in 79) as well as of Varro and of Brutus.

Antiochus completed the return of the Academy from the Skepticism of Arcesilaus and Carneades to a dogmatic position that he identified with that of the Old Academy. He went beyond the final position of his teacher Philo because he abandoned the anti-Stoic polemic maintained by Philo, and hence he is called the head of a Fifth Academy. The doctrine defended by him and attributed to the Old Academy includes many elements of Peripatetic origin, already perceptible in Philo's final position, as well as many Stoic elements taken in part from Panaetius. So Antiochus brought to its conclusion that eclectic and syncretistic tendency that abandoned the precise differences among the various preceding schools and combined many ideas and theories taken from various schools, and especially from the ancient philosophers of the Academy, of the Peripatos, and of the Stoa, a tendency already evident in Panaetius, Posidonius, and Philo of Larissa. This eclecticism, which sought to harmonize and unify the doctrines of the three principal schools, led necessarily to a reinterpretation and modification of the original doctrines, and sometimes introduced doctrines attributed to preceding thinkers but actually new. In the first place, the eclectic Platonism that we encounter in the philosophical and doxographical literature of the first two centuries A.D. (and which in the last decades has been called Middle Platonism) has close ties to Antiochus and his school—even if those ties may be indirect and even though

Antiochus' name is not cited as often as one would expect. But the unanimous attribution to Plato of doctrines that are not found in his authentic writings or in those of his immediate successors must be founded on the authority of a head of the Platonic school, who in this case could be no other than Antiochus.

On the life and historical position of Antiochus we have several sure, though incomplete, testimonies. According to Eusebius, Antiochus was the student of Philo but began another Academy. Studying also with the Stoic Mnesarchus, he assumed a position contrary to his teacher Philo and introduced many foreign ideas into the Academy.[1] Sextus Empiricus says that Antiochus began the Fifth Academy, that he introduced Stoic doctrine into the Academy, and it was said of him that he taught Stoicism within the Academy because he showed that Stoic doctrines are found in Plato himself[2] (a somewhat exaggerated formula, as we shall see). Plutarch, in the *Life of Lucullus*, quotes a passage from Antiochus' book on the gods in which he mentions the battle of Tigranocerta (69 B.C.) and says of Lucullus that he was a friend of the Academy, not of the New Academy of Philo but of the Old Academy, which had as its head Antiochus of Ascalon, a man of persuasion and eloquence.[3] Plutarch also recounts in the *Life of Cicero* that he heard the discourses of Antiochus in Athens and was much impressed by his eloquence and his personality, but did not agree with the doctrinal innovations of the scholarch. At that time Antiochus had already abandoned the

1. Eusebius, *Praeparatio Evangelica* 14.9; G. Luck, *Der Akademiker Antiochos*, fr. 58.

2. Sextus Empiricus, *Pyrrhonianae Dissertationes* 1.220, 235; Luck, fr. 36, 55.

3. Plutarch, *Life of Lucullus* 42; Luck, fr. 15.

so-called New Academy and the sect of Carneades, perhaps changing his mind under the impression of the evidence and perceptions (cited by the Stoics), and perhaps, according to some, also out of ambition and disagreement with the students of Clitomachus and Philo, he adopted a major portion of the Stoic doctrine.[4] Plutarch again, in his *Life of Brutus*, says that Brutus despised the New Academy and followed the Old one, that he admired Antiochus, and had as his private teacher Ariston, Antiochus' brother.[5]

To these testimonies we must add those of Cicero, which are of great value in this case. In the dialogue that bears his name, Cicero has Lucullus say that at the time he was *proquaestor* in Alexandria (in 86 B.C.) Antiochus was with him and received a new book by his teacher Philo and that he composed then a book entitled *Sosus* against Philo.[6] In another passage Cicero has Lucullus say that Antiochus was also with him in Syria shortly before he was to die (in 68).[7] Lucullus relates that Antiochus had followed for a long time the Skeptic doctrines of his teacher Philo, but that he then changed his opinion, criticizing the same Skeptic doctrines that before he had defended and adopting other doctrines, and especially many Stoic doctrines.[8] He then said he had revived the Old Academy, perhaps because he wanted to keep at least the glorious name of the school after having abandoned the substance of its doctrine. Some thought that he was driven by ambition, hoping that his followers would be called Antiochians. But it is probable that he was no longer able to withstand

4. Plutarch, *Life of Cicero* 4; Luck, fr. 12.

5. Plutarch, *Life of Brutus* 2; Luck, fr. 23.

6. Cicero, *Academica Priora* 11–12; Luck, fr. 4.

7. Cic., *Acad. Pr.* 61; Luck, fr. 34.

8. Cic., *Acad. Pr.* 69; Luck, fr. 3.

the criticisms of all other philosophers and so followed in the shade of the ancient Academics.[9] Cicero often calls himself Antiochus' pupil and speaks of him with great respect, while not always following his doctrine.[10] He says explicitly that he heard Antiochus speak for six months at Athens, and he confirms that Antiochus returned from the New Academy to the Old and that he wrote at least one work against his teacher Philo.[11]

So we are sure of the following facts: Antiochus changed his philosophical position; in his first period he followed the so-called New Academy of Carneades and Philo; then he took up a dogmatic position, declared his return from the New Academy to the Old, and accepted several Stoic doctrines. The explanations for his change and the motives given, ambition and weakness, reflect the criticism of his Skeptic adversaries. The testimonies on the real doctrine of Antiochus are neither numerous nor good, but we know that some passages in Cicero, especially in the *Academica Priora* (also called the *Lucullus*) and in the *De finibus,* reflect the position of Antiochus. In the *Academica Priora* it is clearly stated that Lucullus in his discourse is expounding the doctrine of his teacher Antiochus,[12] and Plutarch in his *Life of Lucullus* confirms that Cicero wrote a dialogue in which he attributed to Lucullus the doctrine of Antiochus on comprehension.[13] In the *Academica Posteriora* Cicero has Atticus say that Varro is going to present

9. Cic., *Acad. Pr.* 70; Luck, fr. 3.

10. Cic., *Acad. Pr.* 98, 113; Luck, fr. 51–63.

11. Cicero, *Brutus* 315; Cicero, *De finibus* 5.1; Luck, fr. 8, 10.

12. Cic., *Acad. Pr.* 10.61; Luck, fr. 17, 34.

13. Plut., *Luc.* 42; see Luck, fr. 15. Cicero wrote a dialogue "in which he attributed the discourse on comprehension to Lucullus" [en ho ton huper tes katalepseos logon Loukoullou peritetheken].

the doctrine of his teacher Antiochus and that he will do his best to present it in Latin.[14] And Cicero confirms in a letter to Varro himself that in the dialogue of the *Academica Posteriora* he assigned him the part of Antiochus,[15] and repeats in a letter to Atticus that in his dialogue he had assigned the doctrine of Antiochus to Varro.[16] In another letter to Atticus, Cicero declares that the doctrine of Antiochus is very persuasive and that in his exposition of the doctrine the acuity of the reasoning belongs to Antiochus whereas to Cicero instead belongs the splendor of the Latin discourse.[17]

In the fifth book of the *De finibus*, at the onset Cicero addresses Brutus, saying that the discourse of Piso reflects the position of Antiochus and asks Brutus, who approves of Antiochus and who studied at length with his brother Ariston, to see if Piso correctly expresses Antiochus' doctrine.[18] At the end of the book he repeats that the things said by Piso have been much better expressed by their common friend Antiochus.[19]

For a reconstruction of Antiochus' thought one must depend mostly on the fragments collected by Luck, but according to the passages we have quoted it seems to me legitimate to use the discourses of Lucullus in the dialogue bearing his name, those of Varro in the *Academica Posteriora*, and of Piso in the fifth book of *De finibus*, all based on Antiochus even when his name does not appear in the text. We can add some quotations found in other authors, but all the other sources are of

14. Cicero, *Academica Posteriora* 14; Luck, fr. 29.

15. Cicero, *Epistolae ad Familiares* 9.8; Luck, fr. 22.

16. Cicero, *Epistolae ad Atticum* 13.19.3; Luck, fr. 21.

17. Cic., *Ep. ad Atticum* 13.9.5.

18. Cic., *De fin.* 5.8; Luck, fr. 25.

19. Cic., *De fin.* 5.75; Luck, fr. 79.

dubious value, and I do not set any stock in the fourth book of *De finibus* or the *Tusculanae Disputationes* as sources for the doctrine of Antiochus. Something may be gathered from the consensus of the doxographical sources, as we shall see, but also here one must proceed with great prudence.

In the *Academica Priora* Lucullus takes up the arguments contained in a work of Antiochus entitled *Sosus* and directed against his teacher Philo of Larissa.[20] While Philo had recently defended the Skepticism of Arcesilaus and Carneades, at the same time agreeing with the doctrine of the Old Academy and repeating the Skeptical arguments against the Stoic doctrine of comprehension, Antiochus criticizes Arcesilaus for having destroyed the solid teaching of the Old Academics. Socrates and Plato were in no way Skeptics: Socrates simply hid his doctrine behind irony, and Plato left after himself quite a solid body of doctrine.[21] The Old Academics and Peripatetics had a common doctrine, being distinct only in the words and nomenclature but in agreement with each other on the substance of their doctrine. Even the Stoics differed from the Academics and Peripatetics in their terminology rather than in the substance of their doctrine.[22] Hence, Antiochus is defending what he considers to be the common doctrine of Academics, Peripatetics, and Stoics, and he accepts and reaffirms the Stoic doctrine of comprehension against Arcesilaus, Carneades, and his teacher Philo.[23] Philo is not coherent in his position because he would like to avoid a complete Skepticism, but is not able to do so when he denies comprehension.[24] Sound and valid

20. Cic., *Acad. Pr.* 12; Luck, fr. 4.
21. Cic., *Acad. Pr.* 15.
22. Ibid.
23. Cic., *Acad. Pr.* 17–19.
24. Cic., *Acad. Pr.* 18; Luck, fr. 62.

perception that is not contradicted is the basis of every certainty and truth,[25] and without valid perceptions there would be no memory or knowledge or demonstration, no virtue or wisdom.[26] Even the Skeptic doctrine that nothing can be known must be certain, since every judgment of truth and every moral end depends on it, even for the Skeptics themselves.[27] Therefore, it presupposes the criterion of certainty, and the probability suggested by Carneades is insufficient.[28] Antiochus also defends the Stoic doctrine of assent, since without it no action would be possible.[29] He criticizes the contradiction implicit in the Skeptic doctrine when it states there is no clear difference between true and false perception, not realizing that this same argument presupposes a distinction between the true and the false.[30] Antiochus, following Chrysippus, also tries to refute the Skeptic argument of the identical twins with the postulate of the total individualization of all existing things.[31]

From the second part of the book, which tries to refute Antiochus, we learn other particulars of his doctrine. It is not true that the wise man giving his assent to some perception must have opinions, since he well knows the distinction between true and false and between things that can and cannot be perceived.[32] Antiochus, however, does not agree with the Stoics on all points. Unlike them he does not consider all vices

25. Cic., *Acad. Pr.* 19.
26. Cic., *Acad. Pr.* 22–26.
27. Cic., *Acad. Pr.* 29; Luck, fr. 67.
28. Cic., *Acad. Pr.* 32–33.
29. Cic., *Acad. Pr.* 37–39.
30. Cic., *Acad. Pr.* 111; Luck, fr. 70.
31. Cic., *Acad. Pr.* 57.
32. Cic., *Acad. Pr.* 67.

as equal,[33] and he affirms that virtue alone is the foundation of the happy life, but not the most happy life[34] (an idea that reflects Aristotle's position). Almost all these points of Antiochus' doctrine are repeated with a few additional nuances in the *Academica Posteriora*[35] and in the fifth book of the *De finibus*.[36]

Outside of Cicero we have two passages in Sextus Empiricus that mention Antiochus and are rather brief, but they have the advantage of preserving some elements of his Greek terminology, which is not easy to recognize in the Ciceronian texts. According to Antiochus, phantasy, which is the basis for all knowledge, communicates to us not only itself but also the evident object that produces it. When we see something, we notice the phantasy and also the visible object producing it. As the light shows itself and all things contained in it, so the phantasy, which is the cause of all knowledge, must show itself and also the evident object that produces it.[37] In another passage quoted by Sextus, Antiochus insists that our comprehension is based on perception and not on reasoning.[38]

Antiochus' position is not known to us exactly since Cicero, our principal source, does not preserve the original terminology and often confuses his presentation through inaccuracies and repetitions. Nonetheless, some points hold firm. Antiochus abandoned the original Skeptic and anti-Stoic position of his Academic predecessors and tried to establish a concord

33. Cic., *Acad. Pr.* 133; Luck, fr. 85.

34. Cic., *Acad. Pr.* 134; Luck, fr. 80.

35. Cic., *Acad. Post.* 15–43. See Luck, fr. 48–49.

36. Cic., *De fin.* 5.10–81. See Luck, fr. 40.

37. Sextus Empiricus, *Adversus mathematicos* 7.162–63. See Luck, fr. 65.

38. Sext. Emp., *Adv. math.* 7.201–202; Luck, fr. 66.

among the Old Academics, the Peripatetics, and the Stoics. Many compromises result from this and also many dubious or arbitrary attributions and interpretations with respect to the doctrine of the preceding philosophers. But Antiochus had a very strong influence, and in a certain sense he inaugurated the second period of Hellenistic philosophy. With respect to the preceding age, characterized by the rivalry of the principal schools of Athens, Antiochus introduced an eclecticism that tended to combine different elements of the Platonic, Aristotelian, and Stoic schools in an arbitrary but plausible synthesis, a tendency noticeable in Cicero, who had Antiochus among his teachers, and in many popular authors of the following centuries. One should note, however, that this eclecticism did not include Epicurean or Skeptic doctrines, which continued on their separate ways until the end of classical Antiquity. But Antiochus was the recognized head of the Academic school and had the necessary authority to impose his own doctrine on the Platonists of the following age. I consider him to be the founder of what is called Middle Platonism—that is, of that common doctrine found in Albinus, in the so-called doxographers, in certain passages of Seneca, in Philo of Alexandria, in Origen and others, and which was then absorbed and transformed by the neo-Platonists and by many Christian thinkers.

I admit that one should be very prudent in every attempt to attribute to Antiochus doctrines that are not cited with his name by Cicero, Sextus Empiricus, and other ancient authors. But I want to conclude my discourse with a famous doctrine attributed to Plato himself by the majority of the Middle Platonists and neo-Platonists, but which is not in the least to be found in Plato—indeed, is contrary to Platonic doctrine as we find it in the dialogues. It has been my conviction for many decades that it was Antiochus who invented and proposed such a doctrine, and I consider this attribution as quite probable, if not sure. It is the doctrine of Plato's ideas as thoughts of God.

The ideas of Plato have a separate, absolute, and intelligible existence and have no direct relationship with God, as is clearly seen in the *Timaeus*. The doctrine that Platonic ideas are nothing but concepts or notions of our soul was formulated as an anti-Platonic criticism by Antisthenes,[39] and was known to Plato, who rejects it in the *Parmenides*.[40] As we have seen, the reductionist doctrine of Antisthenes that ideas are simple notions (*ennoiai*) in our soul was accepted and transmitted by Zeno and by Chrysippus and so became a part of orthodox Stoic doctrine.[41] Then we found in the *Orator* of Cicero the doctrine that the perfect orator does not exist in reality but is only in our soul like a Platonic idea, and we suggested that Panaetius, who did not believe in the real existence of the Stoic sage, characterized it as a notion or idea of our soul. In this way he gave an interpretation of Stoic doctrine that, if not Platonic, is at least closer to the thought of Plato, whom Panaetius admired. Then Cicero transferred this concept of the sage to that of the perfect orator, whom he wanted to describe in his rhetoric.[42] The idea as a concept of God seems to be a metaphysical transformation of the idea as a human concept; it is attested by Albinus and by the doxographers, by Philo of Alexandria and Seneca, and was then taken over and transformed by Plotinus and the neo-Platonists, by St. Augustine and many medieval philosophers.

39. *Socraticorum Reliquiae*, ed. G. Giannantoni, vol. 2, p. 375 (Antisthenes, section 5A), fr. 149 (from Simplicius, Ammonius, and Tzetzes). Diogenes Laertius, *Vitae et Placita philosophorum* 6.53.

40. Plato, *Parmenides* 132b.

41. Arnim 1 (Zeno), fr. 65; and Arnim 2 (Chrysippus), fr. 360.

42. Cicero, *Orator* 7–10, see above, pp. 18–19.

This diffusion of the doctrine might already be enough to look for its origin in Antiochus, an authoritative source for many doctrines of Middle Platonism and of neo-Platonism. To attribute to Plato himself a metaphysical doctrine not found in his writings, and to obtain the consensus of various and initially independent authors in favor of this Platonic theory and interpretation, it would take the authority of a head of the Academy, and this head could be none other than Antiochus. He was recent enough to have directly influenced all the respective testimonies. He had led the Academy back from its Skeptic phase to a dogmatic position that claimed to be a return to the Old Academy, but in reality was an eclectic position with many Peripatetic and Stoic elements and was influenced also among others by Panaetius, whose interpretation of the Platonic idea constituted a preparatory step and could serve as a point of departure.[43] Some scholars have suggested that the concept of the idea as the thought of God predates Antiochus, but I do not see any sure testimony that could confirm a hypothesis of the sort.

We also have two other testimonies that make the attribution of the doctrine to Antiochus even more probable, if not sure. In the part of the *Academica Posteriora* that reassumes the logic of Antiochus, we also find a passage on the ideas that is not in the *Academica Priora*. There Varro, who is recounting Antiochus' position, attributes to Plato the conception that the criterion of truth is not in the senses, which lead only to uncertain opinions, but in the mind, which grasps the simple and lasting essences called ideas that are notions or concepts

43. W. Theiler, *Die Vorbereitung des Neuplatonismus* (Berlin: Weidmann, 1930), pp. 37–40. See also Kristeller, review of Theiler's book, in *Deutsche Literaturzeitung* no. 3.3 (1932), col. 438–45; and G. Luck, *Der Akademiker Antiochos*, pp. 24, 28–30.

of the soul. He then mentions the critique of the ideas expressed by Aristotle and the position of Zeno, but he does not seem to abandon Plato's position as he understands it.[44] The concept of the idea expounded here by Antiochus does not affirm the absolute reality of the ideas in the authentic sense of Plato, nor does it characterize the ideas as the thoughts of God, but takes them as valid notions in our mind and therefore follows the doctrine of the ideas as valid notions of the human mind, a position that we know from the *Orator* of Cicero and that we have attributed to Panaetius. The passage is not enough to prove that Antiochus formulated the theory of the ideas as the thoughts of God, but it proves that he knew and accepted the doctrine of the ideas as valid notions of our soul that we have attributed to Panaetius and that could easily lead to the more ambitious theory we are trying to trace.

We have an additional testimony that renders the attribution of the doctrine to Antiochus almost certain. In a passage in *The City of God* [*De civitate Dei*], St. Augustine quotes Varro, who had identified the goddess Minerva with the Platonic idea.[45] As Minerva was born in the head of Jove, the allegory indicates that the Platonic idea had its origin in the head, that is, in the mind of God. Since Varro was the direct disciple of Antiochus, it seems almost certain to me that we must trace to Antiochus himself the doctrine of the ideas as thoughts of God. The concept had enormous influence and is found not only in Plotinus and St. Augustine and in almost all medieval philosophers but, with various transformations, in the Platon-

---

44. Cic., *Acad. Post.* 30–33.

45. St. Augustine, *The City of God* [*De civitate Dei*] 7.28; M. T. Varro, *Antiquitates rerum divinarum*, ed. B. Cardauns, vol. 1, p. 90, fr. 206, and vol. 2, pp. 220–222.

ists of the Renaissance, in Descartes and Spinoza, and even in Kant and Hegel.

We have arrived at the end of our lectures, and I would like to conclude them with an attempt to excuse and to justify the theme I have chosen for this solemn occasion. I have to admit that there is a somewhat personal reason. The philosophy of late Antiquity has been a favorite subject of mine since the time of my dissertation on Plotinus, as well as the topic of many courses given at Columbia University and once even here at the Scuola Normale. Since I have never published the substance of these courses, these lectures have provided me with an occasion and a welcome pretext to revise and publish at least a part of my research.

A series of eight lectures would hardly be able to give an even summary picture of all ancient philosophy after Aristotle—that is, from the followers of Plato and Aristotle down to Plotinus or to Proclus and St. Augustine. Only an ambitious undertaking of such a nature, of which I would not find myself capable, would make it possible to show the vast treasure of concepts and ideas, of knowledge and theories that late Antiquity transmitted to medieval and modern thought and that could serve even contemporary and future thought, were it not for the obstinate tendency—partly due to dogmatic and ideological presuppositions, and partly to total ignorance and to a refusal to learn what one does not yet know—to reduce our whole intellectual heritage to the religious tradition called Judeo-Christian, and perhaps also to Aristotelian philosophy. I am afraid that the continued decadence of our classical and cultural education, perhaps less serious in Italy than elsewhere, will make it increasingly difficult to study even Aristotle and Plato and that in a little while we shall be obliged to limit ourselves to these two great thinkers and forsake the study of other philosophers less great, yet interesting and historically important.

Having to make an even more limited choice within the far too vast area of ancient thought after Aristotle, we decided to focus on a few of the thinkers of the Hellenistic age, namely Epicurus, the Old and Middle Stoics, and the Old and New Academy, because, though they lack the stature of Plotinus, Proclus, or St. Augustine, they follow chronologically after Plato and Aristotle (whose direct followers we have had to omit) and, despite their differences, controversies, and polemics, they share a common territory of problems, concepts, and arguments. Our information on these thinkers is so limited that it has only been possible to present their principal ideas within the short time at our disposal. I do not know whether I have succeeded in choosing the most interesting ideas of these thinkers and in interpreting them correctly. I have made no attempt to adapt the ideas and even the terminology of the ancient thinkers to current fashions (for which I have little regard anyway), nor have I attempted to participate, any more than absolutely necessary, in the erudite controversies that dominate the secondary literature on our subject. I have attempted to cite and interpret correctly the testimonies that are preserved on the single thinkers, since so little survives of the original text of their writings. I have tried to explain the philosophical and historical significance of the principal doctrines, emphasizing the meaning of the terminology, often new or modified, used by our thinkers. There are many nuances we must be aware of, if we want to avoid the mistaken impression that the thinkers of the past were always repeating the same opinions, which anyway were banal or false, or worse, according to certain present opinions.

Our subject has certainly been neglected as of rather marginal interest, and it interests but a small number, even among the specialists in ancient philosophy. It also has no current political or utilitarian significance, a criterion that seems to dominate today the university world internationally, if not that of Italy and of Pisa. I have pursued this theme primarily as an appendix to the history of philosophy and to classical philology, subjects that I have cultivated during my whole life and that seem to me important, although today they are threatened in their very existence by the public and academic fashions that are taking away from our modest enterprise even that relative significance that it still seemed to have a few decades ago.

I hope that the current tendency to look at only what is original or sensational or goes along with the fads of the moment will not last long, and I wish for a renewed respect for the accurate method of philological, historical, and philosophical research: an accuracy that in itself has an intellectual, moral, and aesthetic value and that does not pretend to solve all historical problems at the same time, but to solve some of them step by step, leaving aside those that are either insolvable or at least not solvable at a given moment. But to return to accuracy, one must also return to the modesty that becomes a serious scholar, who must always be conscious of the fact that his person, his vanity and reputation, his academic or political power are worth nothing compared to historical and philosophical truth and to the substance of the writings and thoughts left to us by our predecessors to be understood, rethought, and critically modified.

I do not surrender to the passing fads, and I believe that the serious and methodical study of history, of literature, and of philosophy will not cease. Our subject is not only a secondary supplement vis-à-vis better-known and perhaps more important topics, but is also suited to a study done with accurate and precise methods and based on original sources interpreted according to various degrees of certainty, probability, and possibility. There are subjects (but not for me) that are more interesting and more promising for others, but that cannot be proven or documented. The task of the historian and philologist, to my mind, is to verify, describe, and interpret what can be documented, and not to construct ambitious theories that have no basis in texts or documents. I consider irresponsible and uncritical the Skepticism that accepts as true what cannot be proven and rejects as dubious what can be proven and documented.

Our theme, and the larger theme of which it is a part, namely the history of Western philosophy, is for me a very important subject and one which is part of that history of ideas and of culture that tries to investigate and to understand our intellectual heritage in all its aspects. It encompasses authors and problems of different times and of different importance, among which we can choose those that interest us most. It contains a rich and inexhaustible treasury of valid or at least interesting ideas, each of which occupies a precise place in the history of thought and of philosophical language and which as a whole offers us a richer, more complex, and more interesting picture than the limited and still insufficiently investigated ideas that dominate our present situation.

I do not pretend to have arrived at definitive interpretations and conclusions, but I shall be content if I have succeeded in encouraging some young listeners or readers to acquire and refine the philological, historical, and philosophical methods that permit us to interpret the sources of our past and to apply such methods to themes different from my own, but of interest to them. They should also realize that the past better understood in itself (rather than misunderstood on the basis of an imaginary present and future) can always be useful in our quest for a better vision and a transformation of our present and of our future.

Bibliography

I wish to thank the following scholars for various bibliographical indications: David Ackerman, Uta-Renate Blumenthal, Dieter Bremer, Antonio Gargano, Thomas M. Greene, Maryanne C. Horowitz, James Hankins, Bonnie D. Kent, Dirk Obbink, David Sider, Gisela Striker, and Leonardo Tarán. I also thank Professor Theodore F. Brunner and Professor Richard Frank of the University of California, Irvine, for as yet unpublished information based on the *Thesaurus Linguae Graecae* (computerized printout). Mrs. Julia Rudolf helped me with many references, loans, and photocopies from the Columbia University Library and the Yale University Library.

I. PRIMARY SOURCES: EDITIONS OF TEXTS AND FRAGMENTS

Adorno, F., ed. *Corpus dei papiri filosofici greci e latini. Testi e lessico nei papiri di cultura greca e latina, Autori noti,* vol. 1, parts 1 and 2. Unione Accademica Nazionale, Accademia Toscana di Scienze e Lettere "La Colombaria." Florence: L. S. Olschki, 1989–1992.

Amphinomus. *See* F. Lasserre.

Amyclas. *See* F. Lasserre.

Angeli, A., ed. and trans. *Filodemo: "Agli amici di scuola."* La Scuola di Epicuro, no. 7. Naples: Bibliopolis, 1988.

Antiochus of Ascalon. *See* G. Luck.

Aristippus. *See* G. Giannantoni; E. Mannebach.

Aristo of Ceos. *See* F. Wehrli, *Die Schule des Aristoteles,* vol. 6 (1968).

Aristo the Younger. *See* F. Wehrli, *Die Schule des Aristoteles,* vol. 10 (1969).

Aristoxenus. *See* F. Wehrli, *Die Schule des Aristoteles,* vol. 2 (1967).

Arnim, H. von, ed. *Stoicorum Veterum Fragmenta.* 4 vols. Leipzig: B. G. Teubner, 1903–24; reprint, Stuttgart: B. G. Teubner, 1964.

Arrighetti, G., ed. *Epicuro: Opere.* Turin: G. Einaudi, 1960; 2d ed., 1973.

Asclepiades. *See* F. Lasserre.

Athenaeus of Cyzicus. *See* F. Lasserre.

Bailey, C., ed. and trans. *Epicurus: The Extant Remains.* Oxford: Clarendon Press, 1926.

Bignone, E., ed. *Epicuro: Opere, frammenti, testimonianze.* Bari: G. Laterza, 1920; reprint, Rome: "L'Erma" di Bretschneider, 1964.

Boer, E., ed. and trans. *Epikur: Brief an Pythokles.* Berlin: Akademie-Verlag, 1954.

Brunner, Theodore F. et al., eds. *Thesaurus Linguae Graecae* (computerized printout). Irvine: University of California, n.d.

Caley, E. R. and J. F. C. Richards, eds. and trans. *Theophrastus: On Stones.* Columbus: Ohio State University, 1956.

Capasso, M., ed. and trans. *Carneisco: Il secondo libro del "Filista."* La Scuola di Epicuro, no. 10. Naples: Bibliopolis, 1988.

Carneades. *See* B. Wiśniewski.

Carneiscus. *See* M. Capasso.

Chamaeleo. *See* F. Wehrli, *Die Schule des Aristoteles,* vol. 9 (1969).

Chrysippus. *See* H. von Arnim; K. Hülser.

Cleanthes. *See* H. von Arnim; N. Festa; A. C. Pearson.

Clearchus. *See* F. Wehrli, *Die Schule des Aristoteles,* vol. 3 (1969).

Coriscus. *See* F. Lasserre.

Critolaus. *See* F. Wehrli, *Die Schule des Aristoteles,* vol. 10 (1969).

Cronache Ercolanesi. Vols. 1–16. Naples: G. Macchiaroli, 1971–86.

Cynics. *See* G. Giannantoni; L. Paquet.

Cyrenaics. *See* G. Giannantoni; E. Mannebach.

Decleva Caizzi, F., ed. *Pirrone: Testimonianze.* Naples: Bibliopolis, 1981.

De Lacy, P. H. and E. A. De Lacy, eds. and trans. *Philodemus: On Methods of Inference.* Philadelphia, The American Philological Association, 1941; rev. ed., La Scuola di Epicuro, no. 1, Naples: Bibliopolis, 1978.

Demetrius Laco. *See* E. Puglia; C. Romeo.

Demetrius of Phalerum. *See* F. Wehrli, *Die Schule des Aristoteles,* vol. 4 (1968).

Diano, C., ed. *Epicuri Ethica.* Florence: G. C. Sansoni, 1946.

Dicaearchus. *See* F. Wehrli, *Die Schule des Aristoteles,* vol. 1 (1967).

Diels, H., ed. *Doxographi Graeci.* Berlin: G. Reimer, 1879; reprint, Berlin: W. de Gruyter, 1958.

———, ed. *Poetarum Philosophorum Fragmenta.* Berlin: Weidmann, 1901.

Dinostratus. *See* F. Lasserre.

Diodorus of Tyre. *See* F. Wehrli, *Die Schule des Aristoteles,* vol. 10 (1969).

Dorandi, T., ed. and trans. *Filodemo: Il buon re secondo Omero.* La Scuola di Epicuro, no. 3. Naples: Bibliopolis, 1982.

Döring, K., ed. *Die Megariker, Kommentierte Sammlung der Testimonien.* Amsterdam: Gruener, 1972.

Edelstein, L. and I. G. Kidd, eds. *Posidonius.* Vol. 1, *The Fragments* (including *Testimonia*). Cambridge: Cambridge University Press, 1972.

Eichholz, D. E., ed. and trans. *Theophrastus: De lapidibus.* Oxford: Clarendon Press, 1965.

Einarson, B. and G. K. K. Link, eds. and trans. *Theophrastus: De causis plantarum.* 3 vols. Cambridge, Mass.: Harvard University Press, 1976.

Elis, School of. *See* G. Giannantoni, ed., *Socraticorum Reliquiae,* vol. 1 (1983): section 3, pp. 145–81.

Epicurus. *See* G. Arrighetti; C. Bailey; E. Bignone; E. Boer; C. Diano; M. Isnardi Parente; C. Jensen; W. Schmid; H. Usener; A. Vogliano; P. Von der Muehll; and J. Von Haringer.

Erastus. *See* F. Lasserre.

Eudemus of Rhodes. *See* F. Wehrli, *Die Schule des Aristoteles,* vol. 8 (1969).

Festa, N., ed. *I frammenti degli Stoici antichi.* 2 vols. Bari: G. Laterza, 1932–35.

Fobes, F. M. *See* W. D. Ross; Theophrastus.

Fowler, H. N., ed. *Panaetii et Hecatonis Fragmenta.* Diss., Bonn: C. Georg, 1885.

Giannantoni, G., ed. *I Cirenaici.* Florence: G. C. Sansoni, 1958.

———, ed. *Socraticorum Reliquiae.* 4 vols. Rome: Ateneo, 1983–85.

Graeser, A. *Die logischen Fragmente des Theophrast.* Berlin: W. de Gruyter, 1973.

Hecaton. *See* H. N. Fowler.

Heinze, R. *Xenokrates.* Leipzig: B. G. Teubner, 1892; reprint, Hildesheim: G. Olms, 1965.

Helico. *See* F. Lasserre.

Heraclides Ponticus. *See* F. Wehrli, *Die Schule des Aristoteles,* vol. 7 (1969).

Hermarchus. *See* F. Longo Auricchio.

Hermippus Callimacheus. *See* F. Wehrli, *Die Schule des Aristoteles,* Supplement 1 (1974).

Hermodorus. *See* M. Isnardi Parente; F. Lasserre.

Hermotimus. *See* F. Lasserre.

Hestiaeus. *See* F. Lasserre.

Hieronymus of Rhodes. *See* F. Wehrli, *Die Schule des Aristoteles*, vol. 10 (1969).

Hort, Sir Arthur, ed. and trans. *Theophrastus: De historia plantarum.* 2 vols. Cambridge, Mass.: Harvard University Press, 1916.

Hülser, K., ed. *Die Fragmente zur Dialektik der Stoiker.* 4 vols. Stuttgart–Bad Cannstatt: Frommann-Holzboog, 1987–88.

Indelli, G., ed. and trans. *Filodemo: L'Ira.* La Scuola di Epicuro, no. 5. Naples: Bibliopolis, 1988.

——, ed. and trans. *Polistrato: Sul disprezzo irrazionale delle opinioni popolari.* La Scuola di Epicuro, no. 2. Naples: Bibliopolis, 1978.

Isnardi Parente, M., ed. *Epicuro: Opere.* Turin: Unione Tipografica-Editrice Torinese, 1972; 2d ed., 1983.

——, ed. and trans. *Senocrate, Ermodoro: Frammenti.* La Scuola di Platone, no. 3. Naples: Bibliopolis, 1982.

——, ed. and trans. *Speusippo: Frammenti.* La Scuola di Platone, no. 1. Naples: Bibliopolis, 1980.

Jensen, C. *Ein neuer Brief Epikurs.* Abhandlungen der Gesellschaft der Wissenschaften von Göttingen, Philologisch-historische Klasse, 3. Folge, Nr. 5. Berlin: Weidmann, 1933.

Kidd, I. G. *See* L. Edelstein; Posidonius.

Lang, P., ed. *De Speusippi Academici scriptis.* Diss. Bonn, 1911; reprint, Frankfurt: Minerva, 1964; Hildesheim: G. Olms, 1965.

Lasserre, F., ed. and trans. *De Léodamas de Thase à Philippe d'Oponte.* La Scuola di Platone, no. 2. Naples: Bibliopolis, 1987.

Leo. *See* F. Lasserre.

Leodamas of Thasus. *See* F. Lasserre.

Link, G. K. K. *See* B. Einarson; Theophrastus.

Lloyd-Jones, H. and P. Parsons, eds. *Supplementum Hellenisticum.* Berlin and New York: W. de Gruyter, 1983.

Long, A. A. and D. N. Sedley, eds. and trans. *The Hellenistic Philosophers.* 2 vols. Cambridge: Cambridge University Press, 1987.

Longo Auricchio, F., ed. and trans. *Ermarco: Frammenti.* La Scuola di Epicuro, no. 6. Naples: Bibliopolis, 1988.

Luck, G. *Der Akademiker Antiochos.* Bern: Paul Haupt, 1953.

Lyco. *See* F. Wehrli, *Die Schule des Aristoteles,* vol. 6 (1968).

Mannebach, E., ed. *Aristippi et Cyrenaicorum Fragmenta.* Leiden: E. J. Brill, 1961.

Megarian School. *See* K. Döring; G. Giannantoni, ed., *Socraticorum Reliquiae,* vol. 1 (1983): section 2, pp. 35–143.

Menechmus. *See* F. Lasserre.

Menedemus. *See* F. Lasserre.

Neoclides. *See* F. Lasserre.

Neubecker, A. J., ed. and trans. *Philodemus: Über die Musik, IV. Buch.* La Scuola di Epicuro, no. 4. Naples: Bibliopolis, 1986.

Oates, W. J., ed. *The Stoic and Epicurean Philosophers.* Translated by C. Bailey, P. E. Matheson, H. A. J. Munro, and G. Long. New York: Random House, 1940.

Pamphilus. *See* F. Lasserre.

Panaetius. *See* H. N. Fowler; M. Van Straaten.

Paquet, L., trans. *Les Cyniques grecs, Fragments et témoignages.* Ottawa: Université d'Ottawa, 1975.

Parsons, P. *See* H. Lloyd-Jones; Timon.

Pearson, A. C., ed. *The Fragments of Zeno and Cleanthes.* London: C. J. Clay, 1891.

Phaenias of Eresus. *See* F. Wehrli, *Die Schule des Aristoteles,* vol. 9 (1969).

Philippus of Opus. *See* F. Lasserre; L. Tarán.

Philodemus. *See* F. Adorno; A. Angeli; *Cronache Ercolanesi*; P. H. and E. A. De Lacy; T. Dorandi; G. Indelli; A. J. Neubecker.

Pines, S. *A New Fragment of Xenocrates and Its Implications.* Transactions of the American Philosophical Society, new ser., 51, pt. 2. Philadelphia: American Philosophical Society, 1961.

Polystratus. *See* G. Indelli.

Posidonius. *See* L. Edelstein and I. G. Kidd; W. Theiler.

Praxiphanes. *See* F. Wehrli, *Die Schule des Aristoteles*, vol. 9 (1969).

Puglia, E., ed. and trans. *Demetrio Lacone: Aporie testuali ed esegetiche in Epicuro*. La Scuola di Epicuro, no. 8. Naples: Bibliopolis, 1988.

Pyrrho. *See* F. Decleva Caizzi; *see also* Timon.

Richards, J. F. C. *See* E. R. Caley; Theophrastus.

Rist, J. M., ed. *The Stoics*. Berkeley: University of California Press, 1978.

Romeo, C., ed. and trans. *Demetrio Lacone: La poesia (De poematis)*. La Scuola di Epicuro, no. 9. Naples: Bibliopolis, 1988.

Ross, W. D. and F. M. Fobes, eds. and trans. *Theophrastus: Metaphysics*. Oxford: Clarendon Press, 1929.

Saunders, J. L., trans. *Greek and Roman Philosophy after Aristotle*. New York: Free Press, 1966.

Schmid, W. *Ethica Epicurea (pap. Herc. 1251)*. Leipzig: O. Harrassowitz, 1939.

Scuola di Epicuro, La. 12 vols. Naples: Bibliopolis, 1978–88. Vol. 1 (1978): *Philodemus: On Methods of Inference*, ed. and trans. P. H. and E. A. De Lacy; vol. 2 (1978): *Polistrato: Sul disprezzo irrazionale delle opinioni popolari*, ed. and trans. G. Indelli; vol. 3 (1982): *Filodemo: Il buon re secondo Omero*, ed. and trans. T. Dorandi; vol. 4 (1986): *Philodemus: Über die Musik, IV. Buch*, ed. and trans. A. J. Neubecker; vol. 5 (1988): *Filodemo: L'Ira*, ed. and trans. G. Indelli; vol. 6 (1988): *Ermarco: Frammenti*, ed. and trans. F. Longo Auricchio; vol. 7 (1988): *Filodemo: "Agli amici di scuola,"* ed. and trans. A. Angeli; vol. 8 (1988): *Demetrio Lacone: Aporie testuali ed esegetiche in Epicuro*, ed. and trans. E. Puglia; vol. 9 (1988): *Demetrio Lacone: La poesia (De poematis)*, ed. and trans. C. Romeo; vol. 10 (1988): *Carneisco: Il secondo libro del "Filista,"* ed. and trans. M. Capasso; Vol. 11 (1991): *Polieno: Frammenti*, ed. and trans. A. Tepedino Guerra; vol. 12 (1991): *Filodemo: Storia dei Filosofi, Platone e l'Academia* (PHero. 1021 e 164), ed. and trans. T. Dorandi.

Scuola di Platone, La. 3 vols. Naples: Bibliopolis, 1980–87. Vol. 1 (1980): *Speusippo: Frammenti*, ed. and trans. M. Isnardi Parente; vol.

2 (1987): *De Léodamas de Thase à Philippe d'Oponte*, ed. and trans. F. Lasserre (includes the following authors: Amphinomus, Amyclas, Asclepiades, Athenaeus of Cyzicus, Coriscus, Dinostratus, Erastus, Helico, Hermodorus, Hermotimus, Hestiaeus, Leo, Leodamas of Thasus, Menechmus, Menedemus, Neoclides, Pamphilus, Philippus of Opus, Socrates the Younger, Theaetetus, Theudius); vol. 3 (1982): *Senocrate, Ermodoro: Frammenti*, ed. and trans. M. Isnardi Parente.

Socrates the Younger. *See* F. Lasserre.

Socratics. *See* G. Giannantoni, ed., *Socraticorum Reliquiae*.

Sotio. See F. Wehrli, *Die Schule des Aristoteles*, Supplement 2 (1978).

Speusippus. *See* M. Isnardi Parente; P. Lang; L. Tarán.

Stoics. *See* H. von Arnim; K. Hülser; J. M. Rist.

Strato of Lampsacus. *See* F. Wehrli, *Die Schule des Aristoteles*, vol. 5 (1969).

Tarán, L. *Academica: Plato, Philip of Opus and the Pseudo-Platonic Epinomis.* Philadelphia: American Philosophical Society, 1975.

———. *Speusippus of Athens.* Leiden: E. J. Brill, 1981.

Theaetetus. *See* F. Lasserre.

Theiler, W., ed. *Poseidonios: Die Fragmente.* 2 vols. Berlin and New York: W. de Gruyter, 1982.

Theophrastus. *See* E. R. Caley; D. E. Eichholz; B. Einarson and G. K. K. Link; F. M. Fobes; A. Graeser; Sir Arthur Hort; J. F. C. Richards; W. D. Ross and F. M. Fobes; F. Wimmer.

Theudius. *See* F. Lasserre.

Timon. *See* H. Diels, ed., *Poetarum Philosophorum Fragmenta*; H. Lloyd-Jones and P. Parsons.

Usener, H., ed. *Epicurea.* Bonn: C. Georg, 1881; reprint, Rome: "L'Erma" di Bretschneider, 1963.

Van Straaten, M. *Panétius.* Amsterdam: H. J. Paris, 1946; 2d ed., 1952.

Van Straaten, M., ed. *Panaetii Rhodii Fragmenta.* 3d ed. Leiden: E. J. Brill, 1962.

Bibliography

Varro, M. T. *Antiquitates rerum divinarum*. Edited by B. Cardauns. 2 vols. Mainz: Akademie der Wissenschaften und der Literatur; Wiesbaden: F. Steiner, 1976.

Vogliano, A., "I frammenti del XIV libro del *peri phuseos* di Epicuro." *Rendiconti della R. Accademia delle Scienze di Bologna, Classe di Scienze Morali*, ser. 3, 6 (1931–32): 33–76.

———. *I resti dell'XI libro del "peri phuseos" di Epicuro*. Cairo: Institut français d'archéologie orientale, 1940.

Vogliano, A., ed. *Epicuri et Epicureorum scripta in Herculanensibus papyris servata*. Berlin: Weidmann, 1928.

Von der Muehll, P., ed. *Epicurus: Epistulae tres et ratae sententiae*. Leipzig: B. G. Teubner, 1922.

Von Harringer, J., ed. *Epikur: Fragmente*. Zurich: W. Classen, 1947.

Wehrli, F., ed. *Die Schule des Aristoteles*. 10 vols. Basel: B. Schwabe, 1944–59; 2d. ed., 1967–69; Supplements 1 and 2. Basel: B. Schwabe, 1974, 1978. Vol. 1 (1967): *Dikaiarchos*; vol. 2 (1967): *Aristoxenos*; vol. 3 (1969): *Klearchos*; vol. 4 (1968); *Demetrios von Phaleron*; vol. 5 (1969): *Straton von Lampsakos*; vol. 6 (1968): *Lykon und Ariston von Keos*; vol. 7 (1969): *Herakleides Pontikos*; vol. 8 (1969): *Eudemos von Rhodos*; vol. 9 (1969): *Phainias von Eresos, Chamaileon, Praxiphanes*; vol. 10 (1969): *Hieronymos von Rhodos, Kritolaos, Ariston der jüngere, Diodoros von Tyros*; Supplement 1 (1974): *Hermippos der Kallimacheer*; Supplement 2 (1978): *Sotion*.

Wimmer, F., ed. *Theophrastus: Opera*. 3 vols. Leipzig: B. G. Teubner, 1854–62.

———, ed. *Theophrastus: Opera*. Paris: Didot, 1865; reprint, Frankfurt: Minerva, 1964.

Wiśniewski, B., ed. *Karneades: Fragmente, Text und Kommentar*. Wrocław: Ossolineum, 1970.

Xenocrates. *See* R. Heinze; M. Isnardi Parente; S. Pines.

Zeno. *See* H. von Arnim; N. Festa; A. C. Pearson.

II. SECONDARY LITERATURE

Amand, D. *Fatalisme et liberté dans l'antiquité grecque.* Louvain: Bibliothèque de l'université, 1945.

André, J.-M. See *Aufstieg.*

L'Année philologique. Paris: Les Belles Lettres, 1924–. *See also* J. Marouzeau.

Armstrong, A. H. "The Background of the Doctrine 'That the Intelligibles are not outside the Intellect.' " In *Les Sources de Plotin,* pp. 393–425. Geneva: Fondation Hardt, 1960.

Armstrong, A. H., ed. *The Cambridge History of Later Greek and Early Medieval Philosophy.* Cambridge: Cambridge University Press, 1967. See also *Cambridge History.*

Atanassiévitch, X. *L'Atomisme d'Epicure.* Paris: Presses universitaires de France, 1927.

Aufstieg und Niedergang der Römischen Welt. Edited by H. Temporini and W. Haase. Part I, vol. 4. Berlin and New York: W. de Gruyter, 1973. With contributions by W. Fauth, O. Gigon, E. Paratore, P. L. Schmidt, and G. Verbeke.

———. Part 2, vol. 36, 1 and 2. Berlin and New York: W. de Gruyter, 1987. With contributions by J.-M. André, U. Bianchi, H. J. Blumenthal, F. E. Brenk, L. Brisson, J. Bussanich, K. Corrigan, L. Deitz, J. Dillon, D. A. Dombrowski, P. L. Donini, M. Frede, Ch. Froidefond, H. B. Gottschalk, P. Hadot, J. P. Hershbell, B. L. Hijmans, Jr., K. Kremer, A. Madigan, C. Moreschini, P. O'Cleirigh, F. M. Schroeder, R. W. Sharples, A. Smith, S. K. Strange, D. Tsekourakis, R. T. Wallis, and J. Whittaker.

Bailey, C. *The Greek Atomists and Epicurus.* Oxford: Clarendon Press, 1928; reprint, New York: Russell and Russell, 1964.

Baltes, M. *See* H. Dörrie.

Barnes, J. *See* M. Schofield.

Bianchi, U. See *Aufstieg.*

Bignone, E. *L'Aristotele perduto e la formazione filosofica di Epicuro*. 2 vols. Florence: La Nuova Italia, 1936.

Blume, H.-D. and F. Mann, eds. *Platonismus und Christentum: Festschrift für Heinrich Dörrie*. Jahrbuch für Antike und Christentum, Ergänzungsband 10. Münster: Aschendorff, 1983.

Blumenthal, H. J. See *Aufstieg*.

Bochenski, I. M. *Ancient Formal Logic*. Amsterdam: North-Holland, 1951.

————. *Elementa logicae Graecae*. Rome: Anonima Libraria Cattolica Italiana, 1937.

————. *Formale Logik*. Freiburg: K. Alber, 1956.

————. *La Logique de Théophraste*. Fribourg: Librairie de l'université, 1947.

Bréhier, E. *Chrysippe*. Paris: Alcan, 1910.

————. *Chrysippe et l'ancien stoïcisme*. Paris: Presses universitaires de France, 1951.

————. *Histoire de la philosophie*. Vol. 1. Paris: Presses universitaires de France, 1938; 9th ed., Paris: 1967.

Brenk, F. E. See *Aufstieg*.

Brisson, L. See *Aufstieg*.

Brochard, V. *Les Sceptiques grecs*. Paris: Imprimerie Nationale, 1887; 2d ed., Paris: J. Vrin, 1932.

Burnyeat, M. *The Skeptical Tradition*. Berkeley: University of California Press, 1983.

————. *See* M. Schofield.

Bussanich, J. See *Aufstieg*.

Cambridge History of Later Greek and Early Medieval Philosophy, The. Edited by A. H. Armstrong. Cambridge: Cambridge University Press, 1967. With contributions by C. Chadwick, A. C. Lloyd, R. A. Markus, P. Merlan, and I. P. Sheldon-Williams.

Capizzi, A. *See* E. Zeller, *La filosofia dei greci*.

Cesa, C. *See* E. Zeller, *La filosofia dei greci*.

Chadwick, H. See *The Cambridge History of Later Greek and Early Medieval Philosophy*.

Cherniss, H. *The Riddle of the Early Academy*. Berkeley: University of California Press, 1945.

Christensen, J. *An Essay on the Unity of Stoic Philosophy*. Copenhagen: Munksgaard, 1962.

Cione, E. *See* E. Panofsky.

Clark, G. H., trans. *Selections from Hellenistic Philosophy*. New York: F. S. Crofts, 1940.

Classen, C. J. *See* R. Philippson.

Cleary, J. *See* G. Striker.

Colish, M. L. *The Stoic Tradition from Antiquity to the Early Middle Ages*. 2 vols. Leiden: E. J. Brill, 1985.

Copleston, F. *History of Philosophy*. Vol. 1: *Greece and Rome*. Westminster, Md.: Newman Press, 1950.

Corrigan, K. See *Aufstieg*.

De Ruggiero, G. *Storia della filosofia*. 2 vols. Bari: Laterza, 1920; 4th ed., 1943–48.

De Vogel, C. J. *Greek Philosophy*. 3 vols. Leiden: E. J. Brill, 1950–59.

———. "On the Neoplatonic Character of Platonism and the Platonic Character of Neoplatonism." *Mind* 62 (1953): 43–64.

———. "La recherche des étapes précises entre Platon et le néo-platonisme." *Mnemosyne* 4, no. 7 (1954): 111–22.

De Witt, N. W. *Epicurus and His Philosophy*. Minneapolis: University of Minnesota Press, 1954.

Deitz, L. See *Aufstieg*.

Del Re, R. *See* E. Zeller, *La filosofia dei greci*.

Diano, C. *Scritti epicurei*. Florence: L. S. Olschki, 1974.

Dihle, A. "Science et philosophie à l'époque hellénistique." *Académie des Inscriptions et Belles-Lettres, Comptes Rendus* (1987): 655–66.

Dillon, J. M. *The Middle Platonists*. Ithaca, N.Y.: Cornell University Press, 1977.

———. See also *Aufstieg*.

Dombrowski, D. A. See *Aufstieg.*

Donini, P. *Le scuole, l'anima, l'impero, la filosofia antica da Antioco a Plotino.* Turin: Rosenberg and Sellier, 1982.

———. See also *Aufstieg.*

Döring, K. *Der Sokratesschüler Aristipp und die Kyrenaiker.* Mainz: Akademie der Wissenschaften und der Literatur, Abhandlungen der Geistes—und Sozialwissenschaftlichen Klasse; Wiesbaden: F. Steiner, 1988.

Dörrie, H. *Platonica Minora.* Studia et Testimonia Antiqua, no. 8. Munich: W. Fink, 1976.

———. *See also* H.-D. Blume and F. Mann.

Dörrie, H., with M. Baltes and F. Mann. *Die geschichtlichen Wurzeln des Platonismus.* Der Platonismus in der Antike, no. 1. Stuttgart–Bad Cannstatt: Frommann-Holzboog, 1987.

Doty, R. E. "Early Academic Critique of the Stoic Criterion of Truth." Ph.D. diss., Columbia University, 1973. Published as R. E. Doty, *The Criterion of Truth.* American University Studies, ser. 5, vol. 108. New York: P. Lang, 1992.

Dudley, D. R. *A History of Cynicism.* London: Methuen, 1937.

Duhem, P. *Le Système du monde.* 10 vols. Paris: A. Hermann, 1913–59.

———. *Sozein ta phainomena: Essai sur la notion de théorie physique de Platon à Galilée.* Paris: A. Hermann, 1908. Originally published in *Annales de Philosophie Chrétienne,* 4th ser., 6, no. 155 (1908): 113–39; 277–302, 352–77, 482–514, 561–92.

Dumont, J.-P. *Le Scepticisme et le phénomène: Essai sur la signification et les origines du pyrrhonisme.* Paris: J. Vrin, 1972.

Englert, W. G. *Epicurus on the Swerve and Voluntary Action.* Atlanta: Scholars Press, 1987.

Fauth, W. See *Aufstieg.*

Flashar, H. *See* F. Überweg.

Frede, M. *Die stoische Logik.* Abhandlungen der Göttinger Akademie der Wissenschaften, Philologisch-Historische Klasse, ser. 3, no. 88 (1974). Göttingen: Vanderhoeck and Ruprecht, 1974.

————. See also *Aufstieg.*

Gaiser, K. *Platons ungeschriebene Lehre. Studien zur systematischen und geschichtlichen Begründung der Wissenschaften in der Platonischen Schule.* Stuttgart: E. Klett, 1963; 2d. ed., 1968.

Giannantoni, G. *La scienza ellenistica.* Naples: Bibliopolis, 1984.

Gigante, M. *Ricerche filodemee.* Naples: G. Macchiaroli, 1969.

————. *See also* Pugliese Carratelli; H. Usener, *Glossarium.*

Gigon, O. See *Aufstieg.*

Glucker, J. *Antiochus and the Late Academy.* Hypomnemata 56. Göttingen: Vandenhoeck and Ruprecht, 1976.

Goldschmidt, V. *La Doctrine d'Epicure et le droit.* Paris: J. Vrin, 1977.

Gottschalk, H. B. See *Aufstieg.*

Gould, J. B. *The Philosophy of Chrysippus.* Leiden: E. J. Brill; Albany: State University of New York Press, 1970.

Graeser, A. *Plotinus and the Stoics.* Leiden: E. J. Brill, 1972.

Haase, W. See *Aufstieg.*

Hadot, P. See *Aufstieg.*

Hagius, H. "The Stoic Theory of the Parts of Speech." Ph.D. diss., Columbia University, 1979.

Heimsoeth, H. *See* W. Windelband.

Heinemann, I. *Poseidonios' metaphysische Schriften.* 2 vols. Breslau: M. and H. Marcus, 1921–28.

Hershbell, J. P. See *Aufstieg.*

Hijmans, Jr., B. L. See *Aufstieg.*

Horowitz, M. C. "The Stoic Synthesis of the Natural Law in Man: Four Themes." *Journal of the History of Ideas* 35 (1974): 5–16.

Hunt, H. A. K. *A Physical Interpretation of the Universe: The Doctrines of Zeno the Stoic.* Carlton: Melbourne University Press, 1976.

Isnardi Parente, M. *La filosofia dell'ellenismo.* Turin: Loescher, 1977.

————. *Studi sull'Accademia Platonica antica.* Florence: L. S. Olschki, 1979.

————. *See also* E. Zeller, *La filosofia dei greci.*

Jones, R. M. "The Ideas as the Thoughts of God." *Classical Philology* 21 (1926): 317–26.

Kennedy, G. *The Art of Persuasion in Greece.* Princeton: Princeton University Press, 1963.

———. *The Art of Rhetoric in the Roman World.* Princeton: Princeton University Press, 1972.

———. *Classical Rhetoric and Its Christian and Secular Tradition from Ancient to Modern Times.* Chapel Hill: University of North Carolina Press, 1980.

———. *Greek Rhetoric Under Christian Emperors.* Princeton: Princeton University Press, 1983.

Kent, B. D. "Aristotle and the Franciscans." Ph.D. diss., Columbia University, 1984.

Konstan, D. *Some Aspects of Epicurean Psychology.* Leiden: E. J. Brill, 1973.

Krämer, H. J. *Der Ursprung der Geistmetaphysik.* Amsterdam: Schippers, 1964.

———. *Platonismus und Hellenistische Philosophie.* Berlin: W. de Gruyter, 1971.

———. *See also* F. Überweg, vol. 3, ed. H. Flashar.

Kremer, K. See *Aufstieg.*

Kristeller, P. O. "De formarum sive idearum apud Ciceronem notione." Seminar thesis. University of Berlin, 1929 (unpublished).

———. *Die Ideen als Gedanken der menschlichen und göttlichen Vernunft.* Sitzungsberichte der Heidelberger Akademie der Wissenschaften, Philosophisch-historische Klasse, no. 2 (1989), Heidelberg: Carl Winter, 1989.

———. Review of *Die Vorbereitung des Neuplatonismus,* by W. Theiler. *Deutsche Literaturzeitung* 3, no. 2 (1931): 57–61.

Krokiewicz, A. *Aristoteles, Pirron i Plotyn.* Warsaw: Pax, 1974.

Labowsky, L. *Die Ethik des Panaitios.* Leipzig: F. Meiner, 1934.

Laffranque, M. *Poseidonios d'Apamée.* Paris: Presses universitaire de France, 1964.

Lausberg, H. *Handbuch der literarischen Rhetorik.* 2 vols. Munich: M. Hueber, 1960.

Lloyd, A. C. See *The Cambridge History of Later Greek and Early Medieval Philosophy.*

Lloyd, G. E. R. *Greek Science After Aristotle.* London: Chatto and Windus, 1973.

Loenen, J. H. "Albinus' Metaphysics: An Attempt at Reconciliation." *Mnemosyne* 4, no. 9 (1956): 296–319; no. 10 (1957): 35–56.

Long, A. A. *Hellenistic Philosophy.* London: Duckworth, 1974; 2d. ed., Berkeley: University of California Press, 1986.

———. *Problems in Stoicism.* London: Athlone Press, 1971.

Luck, G. *Arcana Mundi: Magic and the Occult in the Greek and Roman Worlds.* Baltimore: Johns Hopkins University Press, 1985.

Lueder, A. "Die philosophische Persönlichkeit des Antiochos von Askalon." Ph.D. diss., University of Göttingen, 1940.

Madigan, A. See *Aufstieg.*

Mann, F. *See* H. Blume; H.-D. Dörrie.

Mannheimer, A. *Die Ideenlehre bei den Sokratikern, Xenokrates und Aristoteles.* Göttingen: Vandenhoeck and Ruprecht, 1875.

Markus, R. A. See *The Cambridge History of Later Greek and Early Medieval Philosophy.*

Marouzeau, J., ed. *Dix années de bibliographie classique (1914–1924).* 2 vols. Paris: Les Belles Lettres, 1927–28.

Marrou, H. I. *Histoire de l'Éducation dans l'antiquité.* Paris: Editions du Seuil, 1948.

Martano, R. G. *See* E. Zeller, *La filosofia dei greci.*

Martin, J. *Antike Rhetorik.* Munich: C. H. Beck, 1974.

Mates, B. *Stoic Logic.* Berkeley: University of California Press, 1953.

Merlan, P. *From Platonism to Neoplatonism.* The Hague: Martinus Nijhoff, 1953; 2d ed., 1960; 3d ed., 1969.

———. *Studies in Epicurus and Aristotle.* Wiesbaden: O. Harrassowitz, 1960.

————. See also *The Cambridge History of Later Greek and Early Medieval Philosophy*.

Michel, A. *Rhétorique et philosophie chez Cicéron*. Paris: Presses universitaires de France, 1960.

Mondolfo, R. *See* E. Zeller, *La filosofia dei greci*.

More, P. E. *Hellenistic Philosophies*. Princeton: Princeton University Press, 1923.

Moreau, J. *Aristote et son école*. Paris: Presses universitaires de France, 1962.

Moreschini, C. See *Aufstieg*.

Musti, D. *See* E. Zeller, *La filosofia dei greci*.

Neuhausen, K. A. "Academicus Sapiens, Zum Bild des Weisen in der Neuen Akademie." *Mnemosyne* 4, no. 40 (1987): 353–90.

Niehues-Pröbsting, H. *Der Kynismus des Diogenes und der Begriff des Zynismus*. Munich: W. Fink, 1979.

Norden, E. *Die Antike Kunstprosa*. Leipzig: B. G. Teubner, 1898; 5th ed., Stuttgart: B. G. Teubner, 1958.

O'Cleirigh, P. See *Aufstieg*.

Oxford Studies in Ancient Philosophy. Vols. 1 and 2. Oxford: Clarendon Press, 1983–87.

Paleikat, G. *Die Quellen der akademischen Skepsis*. Ph.D. diss., University of Königsberg [Kaliningrad]; published Greifswald: Abel, 1916.

Panofsky, E. *Idea*. Berlin: B. G. Teubner, 1924; 2d ed., Berlin: B. Hessling, 1960; Italian ed. (trans. E. Cione), Florence: La Nuova Italia, 1952; English ed. (trans. J. J. S. Peake), Columbia: University of South Carolina Press, 1968.

Paratore, E. See *Aufstieg*.

Peake, J. J. S. *See* E. Panofsky.

Pfeiffer, R. *History of Classical Scholarship: From the Beginnings to the End of the Hellenistic Age*. Oxford: Clarendon Press, 1968.

Philippson, R. "Nachtrag zu den Panaetiana." *Rheinisches Museum* 79 (1930): 400–10.

———. "Panaetiana." *Rheinisches Museum* 78 (1929): 337–60.

———. "Zur Psychologie der Stoa." *Rheinisches Museum* 86 (1937): 150–79.

———. "Das Sittlichschöne bei Panaitios." *Philologus* 85, N.S. 39 (1929): 357–413.

———. *Studien zu Epikur und den Epikureern*. Edited by W. Schmid and C. J. Classen. Hildesheim: G. Olms, 1983.

Plebe, A. *See* E. Zeller, *La filosofia dei greci*.

Pocar, E. *See* E. Zeller, *La filosofia dei greci*.

Pohlenz, M. *Die Stoa*. 2 vols. Göttingen: Vandenhoeck and Ruprecht, 1948–49.

———. *Stoa und Stoiker*. 2d ed. Zurich: Artemis Verlag, 1950.

Poncelet, R. "Cicéron traducteur de Platon." Ph.D. diss., University of Paris, 1953.

Popkin, R. H. *The History of Scepticism from Erasmus to Descartes*. Assen: Van Gorcum, 1960; rev. ed., 1964.

———. *The History of Scepticism from Erasmus to Spinoza*. Berkeley: University of California Press, 1979.

Prächter, K. *See* F. Überweg.

Prantl, C. *Geschichte der Logik im Abendlande*. Vol. 1. Leipzig: S. Hirzel, 1855.

Pugliese Carratelli, G., ed. *Sunzetesis, Studi sull'Epicureismo greco e romano offerti a M. Gigante*. 2 vols. Naples: G. Macchiaroli, 1983.

Randall, J. H., Jr. *Hellenistic Ways of Deliverance and the Making of the Christian Synthesis*. New York: Columbia University Press, 1970.

Reale, G. *Storia della filosofia antica*. 5 vols. Milan: Vita e pensiero, 1975–80; 4th ed., 1982.

———. *See also* E. Zeller, *La filosofia dei greci*.

Reiley, K. C. *Studies in the Philosophical Terminology of Lucretius and Cicero*. New York: Columbia University Press, 1909.

Reinhardt, K. *Poseidonios*. Munich: C. H. Beck, 1921.

———. *Kosmos und Sympathie*. Munich: C. H. Beck, 1926.

Reitzenstein, E. *Theophrast bei Epikur und Lukrez.* Heidelberg: Carl Winter, 1924.

Repici, L. *La logica di Teofrasto.* Bologna: Il Mulino, 1977.

Rich, A. N. M. "The Platonic Ideas as the Thoughts of God." *Mnemosyne* 4, no. 7 (1954): 123—33.

Rist, J. *Stoic Philosophy.* London: Cambridge University Press, 1969.

————. *Epicurus.* Cambridge: Cambridge University Press, 1972.

Sambursky, S. *Physics of the Stoics.* New York: Macmillan, 1959.

Sandbach, F. H. *The Stoics.* New York: Norton, 1975.

Sandys, Sir Edwin. *A History of Classical Scholarship.* Vol. 1, *From the Sixth Century B.C. to the End of the Middle Ages.* 2d ed. Cambridge: Cambridge University Press, 1906.

Sarton, G. *Introduction to the History of Science.* Vol. 1. Baltimore: Williams and Wilkins, 1927.

Sayre, F. *Diogenes of Sinope.* Baltimore: J. H. Furst, 1938.

Schmekel. A. *Die Philosophie der mittleren Stoa in ihrem geschichtlichen Zusammenhang dargestellt.* Berlin: Weidmann, 1892.

Schmid, W. *Epikurs Kritik der platonischen Elementenlehre.* Leipzig: O. Harrassowitz, 1936.

————. *See also* R. Philippson, *Studien;* Usener, *Glossarium.*

Schmidt, P. L. See *Aufstieg.*

Schofield, M., M. Burnyeat, and J. Barnes. *Doubt and Dogmatism: Studies in Hellenistic Epistemology.* Oxford: Clarendon Press, 1980.

Schofield, M. and G. Striker. *Studies in Hellenistic Ethics.* Cambridge: Cambridge University Press, 1986.

Schroeder, F. M. See *Aufstieg.*

Sedley, D. "Epicurus' Refutation of Determinism." In G. Pugliese Carratelli, ed., *Synzetesis, Studi sull'Epicureismo greco e romano offerti a M. Gigante,* pp. 11–51. Naples: G. Macchiaroli, 1983.

Sharples, R. W. See *Aufstieg.*

Sheldon-Williams, I. P. See *The Cambridge History of Later Greek and Early Medieval Philosophy.*

Smith, A. See *Aufstieg*.

Solmsen, F. *Aisthesis in Aristotelian and Epicurean Thought*. Nederlandse Akademie, Letterkunde, n.s. 2, no. 8. Amsterdam: North Holland, 1961.

Spanneut, M. *Le Stoïcisme des Pères de l'Eglise de Clément de Rome à Clément d'Alexandrie*. Paris: Editions du Seuil, 1957.

Strange, S. K. See *Aufstieg*.

Striker, G. "Origins of the Concept of Natural Law." In J. Cleary, ed., *Proceedings of the Boston Area Colloquium in Ancient Philosophy* 2: 79–94. Lanham, Md.: University Press of America, 1987.

————. *See also* M. Schofield.

Strodach, G.K. *The Philosophy of Epicurus*. Evanston, Ill.: Northwestern University Press, 1963.

Stroux, J. *De Theophrasti virtutibus dicendi*. Leipzig: B. G. Teubner, 1912.

Tarrant, H. *Scepticism or Platonism? The Philosophy of the Fourth Academy*. Cambridge: Cambridge University Press, 1985.

Tatakis, B. N. *Panétius de Rhodes*. Paris: J. Vrin, 1931.

Temporini, H. See *Aufstieg*.

Theiler, W. *Die Vorbereitung des Neuplatonismus*. Berlin: Weidmann, 1930; 2d ed., 1964. (*See also* P. O. Kristeller.)

Thorndike, L. *A History of Magic and Experimental Science*. Vol. 1. New York: Columbia University Press, 1923.

Totok, W. *Handbuch der Geschichte der Philosophie*. Vol. 1. Frankfurt: V. Klostermann, 1964.

Trouard, Sister M. A. "Cicero's Attitude Towards the Greeks." Ph.D. diss., University of Chicago, 1942.

Tsekourakis, D. See *Aufstieg*.

Überweg, F. *Grundriss der Geschichte der Philosophie*. Vol. 1, *Die Philosophie des Altertums*. 12th ed. Edited by K. Prächter. Berlin: E. S. Mittler, 1926.

————. Vol. 3, *Die Philosophie der Antike*. Edited by H. Flashar. With contributions by H. J. Krämer and F. Wehrli. Basel: B. Schwabe, 1983.

Usener, H. *Glossarium Epicureum*. Edited by M. Gigante and W. Schmid. Rome: Ateneo and Bizzarri, 1977.

Valente, M. *L'Ethique Stoïcienne chez Cicéron*. Paris: Librairie Saint-Paul, 1956.

Verbeke, G. *L'Evolution de la doctrine du pneuma du stoïcisme à S. Augustin*. Louvain: Institut supérieur de Philosophie, 1945.

————. *Kleanthes van Assos*. Koninklijke Vlaamse Academie voor Wetenschapen, Klasse der Letteren 11, no. 9 Brussels: Paleis der Academiën, 1949.

————. *The Presence of Stoicism in Medieval Thought*. Washington, D.C.: Catholic University of America Press, 1983.

————. See also *Aufstieg*.

Vick, C. *Quaestiones Carneadeae*. Rostock: M. Warkentien, 1901.

Von Fritz, K. *Quellenuntersuchungen zu Leben und Philosophie des Diogenes von Sinope*. Philologus, Supplement 18, 2. Leipzig: Dieterich, 1926.

————. "Zur antisthenischen Erkenntnistheorie und Logik." *Hermes* 62 (1927): 453–84.

Waddington, C. *Pyrrhon et le Pyrrhonisme*. Académie des sciences morales et politiques, Comptes rendus. Paris: A. Picard, 1876.

Wallis, R. T. See *Aufstieg*.

Wehrli, F., ed. *Das Erbe der Antike*. Zurich: Artemis Verlag, 1963.

————. *See also* F. Überweg, vol. 3, ed. H. Flashar.

Weische, A. *Cicero und die Neue Akademie*. Münster: Aschendorff, 1961.

Wellmann, E. *See* E. Zeller.

Whittaker, J. See *Aufstieg*.

Windelband, W. *Lehrbuch der Geschichte der Philosophie*. 13th ed. Edited by H. Heimsoeth. Tübingen: J. C. B. Mohr, 1935.

Witt, R. E. A. *Albinus and the History of Middle Platonism*. Cambridge,

Cambridge University Press, 1937; reprint, Amsterdam: A. M. Hakkert, 1971.

Wolfson, H. A. *Religious Philosophy*. Cambridge: Harvard University Press, 1961.

Zeller, E. *Die Philosophie der Griechen* (Vol. 3, sec. 1–2: *Die Nacharistotelische Philosophie*). 5th ed. Edited by E. Wellmann. Leipzig: O. R. Reisland, 1923.

―――. *La filosofia dei greci*. Numerous volumes to date (incomplete). Edited by A. Capizzi, C. Cesa, R. Del Re, M. Isnardi Parente, R. G. Martano, R. Mondolfo, D. Musti, A. Plebe, E. Pocar, and G. Reale. Florence: La Nuova Italia, 1923–1979.

Index of *Greek* and Latin Terms

Index of Greek and Latin Terms

Index of Names

(Initials are given for modern scholars.)

Designer : Richard Hendel

Text : 10/15 Palatino

Compositor : Maple Vail Book Manufacturing, Inc.

Printer : Maple Vail Book Manufacturing, Inc.

Binder : Maple Vail Book Manufacturing, Inc.